# GERMAN KNIGHTS OF THE AIR

## 1914–1918

### THE HOLDERS OF THE *ORDEN POUR LE MÉRITE*

TERRY C. TREADWELL
& ALAN C. WOOD

BARNES
&NOBLE
BOOKS
NEW YORK

1998 Barnes & Noble Books

ISBN 0-7607-0790-1

Printed and bound in the United States of America

98 99 00 01 02 MC 10 9 8 7 6 5 4 3 2 1

MV

# Contents

# Acknowledgements

Jack Bruce for his advice and guidance.

Chaz Bowyer for the use of his extensive knowledge of First World War aviation.

Wendy Treadwell for reading and correcting the manuscript and ensuring that everything was grammatically correct.

Neal O'Connor for supplying the photographs of five of the most obscure holders of the *Pour le Mérite*.

Clint Hackney for his generosity in supplying us with a copy of his book *The* Pour le Mérite *and Germany's First Aces*.

Nor law, nor duty bade me fight,
Nor public men, nor cheering crowds,
A lonely impulse of delight
Drove to this tumult in the clouds:
I balanced all, brought all to mind,
The years to come seemed waste of breath,
A waste of breath the years behind
In balance with this life, this death.

*Yeats*

# Historical Introduction

The word 'knight' is derived from the Saxon word '*Cniht*' meaning 'a servant', but came to mean someone who was a member of the king's personal bodyguard, pledged with unswerving loyalty to the sovereign even unto death.

The word knight is historically defined as a military follower, usually of noble birth, who served as a page to the esquire before being raised by king or church to knighthood. The church encouraged the chivalrous ideals of the feudal system – a religious, moral and social code of usage and conduct. The knight was expected to be brave, honourable and courteous to both friend and foe.

Throughout Europe during the eleventh and fourteenth centuries the idea of the chivalrous knight evolved – in part due to the writers who romanticised the state of knighthood into fiction. The Knights of the Teutonic Order – a religious and military order of St Mary's Hospital, Jerusalem – was founded at Acre in 1190 by German Crusaders. The Teutonic Knights (*Deutschritter*) wore white mantles emblazoned with a black cross and fought so well in the Crusades that they were invited early in the thirteenth century to undertake the conquest of Prussia and colonise lands to the east. Becoming powerful they became part of the aristocracy of Prussia and beyond. When the Order of the Knights Templar was suppressed in France in 1312, the German Templars joined the Teutonic Knights of Prussia and in 1522 repudiated their allegiance to Rome and threw their support behind Martin Luther.

During feudal times the power of the church was almost equal to that of the sovereign, and the church tried to teach the ideals of decent conduct in war toward an opponent – a sort of mutual understanding of fair play between adversaries. Needless to say this code of conduct was not always followed – savage acts of war were perpetrated by some knights (and other soldiers) acting on the orders of the church and/or state. A prime example is the so-called Albigensian Crusade of 1209 when a northern army of 30,000 knights and soldiers – acting specifically on the orders of the church – fell on Languedoc in southern France and slaughtered the whole population of men, women and children without mercy, in a war which lasted for nearly 40 years.

But the ideals of knighthood persisted and evolved into chivalrous behaviour by most soldiers, sailors and later airmen. This was based on a mutual understanding that one should not cause unnecessary suffering to an adversary and should spare the innocents in war.

To their credit these ideals were practised by most participants during the First World War and the German Air Service did have a code of honour which demonstrated some of the chivalrous qualities of the knight. There is on record the courteous behaviour of the German fighter pilots toward a downed adversary. If alive he was treated with respect and kindness – if dead he was accorded a burial with full military honours. The Allied air services were equally chivalrous – when Manfred von Richthofen was shot down and killed, he was accorded a Guard of Honour with reversed rifles and a full military funeral.

In order to understand the complexities of the various German kingdoms, principalities and states at this time and their unified approach to the First World War, it may help to explain the way they developed and also kept, to a certain degree, their own identities.

*Oberleutnant Georg Felmy with one of his captured opponents, Lieutenant C Vautin.*

The German First Reich followed the Franco-Prussian War of 1870–71, with the German states continuing their process of unification to counterbalance the power of Russia, France and Austro-Hungary. The then King of Prussia became the first Kaiser (German Emperor) with the new Germany being given a Federal Constitution. The new German Empire was created and proclaimed in the Hall of Mirrors at Versailles in 1871. For the first time since the Middle Ages, the mass of German-speaking people of Europe would be united in a single state.

The new German Empire was a confederation of 26 states: the Kingdoms of Prussia, Bavaria, Saxony and Württemberg; the Grand Duchies of Baden, Hesse, Mecklenburg-Schwerin, Mecklenburg-Strelitz, Saxe-Weimar and Oldenburg; the Duchies of Anhalt, Brunswick, Saxe-Altenberg, Saxe-Coburg-Gotha and Saxe-Meiningen; the Principalities of Lippe, Ruess-Greiz, Ruess-Schleiz, Schaumburg Lippe, Schwarzburg-Rudolstadt, Schwarzburg-Sondershausen and Waldeck; the territory of Alsace-Lorraine and the cities of Bremen, Lubeck and Hamburg. By 1910 the population of Germany had risen to 65 million with Prussia having over 40 million.

*Funeral cortège of Rittmeister Manfred von Richthofen by Australian soldiers with their rifles reversed out of respect.*

The first Kaiser, Wilhelm I, ruled over Germany from 1871 to 1888, being followed by Friedrich III during 1888 and finally by Wilhelm II from 1888 until 1918. These three were members of the aristocratic Prussian House of the Hohenzollern dynasty which was descended from Frederick the Great.

Within the Federal Constitution some armies were under the control of the Prussian Army, but some, the Royal Armies of Saxony and Württemberg, retained their own War Ministries, Headquarters Staff and Establishments. The Royal Bavarian Army remained autonomous under the command of its king, with its own Headquarters Staff and Headquarters Establishment. The various military forces of the smaller states and provinces became integrated with the Prussian Army. At the outbreak of the First World War, however, the military forces of the Imperial German Empire were under unified command with only Bavaria maintaining a separate establishment.

Each of the Kingdoms, States and others had their own range of Orders, Decorations and Medals which they awarded to their subjects and others to whom they saw fit to reward. But only the *Pour le Mérite*, the Golden Military Service Cross (*Militärverdienstkreuz*) and the Iron Cross 1st and 2nd Class, were awarded by Imperial Germany.

The *Brandenburg Ordre de la Génerosité* (Order of Generosity) was founded in 1667 by Friedrich I of Prussia (The Great Elector), but was revised as *Orden Pour le Mérite* by Friedrich II ('Friedrich the Great') on 6 June 1740. It became known colloquially as the Order of Merit in 1740 and was awarded for both civil and military distinguished service. The first recipients of the *Pour le Mérite* were Oberstleutnant Friedrich Wilhelm Marquis de Varenne, Oberst Hans von Hacke and Sammual von Marschall, a State Minister, who were

The Pour le Mérite

given the award at the end of June 1740. By the end of the decade the number of those awarded the *Pour le Mérite* had reached over 300 and among them was the French philosopher Voltaire, who was a friend and confidant of Friedrich II. On 25 September 1750, Voltaire was the first to be awarded the *Pour le Mérite* with *Brilliants* (diamonds) and to receive a yearly pension – an honour that was rescinded some two years later after a disagreement, which resulted in Voltaire being ordered out of Prussia.

In 1810 the qualification changed and the Order was reserved solely for those who achieved military merit against an enemy in the field. The alliance between Prussia and Russia during the war against Napoleon was to see a large number of *Pour le Mérites* being awarded after the Prussian Army had marched into Paris in March 1814. Out of a total of 1,662 awarded, a staggering 1,470 were given to Russians; of these 61 were awarded twice and two given three times. The Order was worn around the neck hung from a black ribbon with stripes of white interwoven with silver towards each edge. The decoration was in the shape of a Maltese Cross in blue enamel, edged with gold and with four Prussian eagles between the limbs. On the upper arm of the Cross was the letter 'F' in gold surmounted by a crown and on the other three arms '*Pour-le Mé-rite*'. When King Friedrich Wilhelm III's wife, Queen Louise of Mecklenburg-Strelitz, died on 19 July 1810, he ordered that oak leaves were to be added to the *Pour le Mérite* and by doing so created a higher award in honour of his wife. The first *Pour le Mérite* with Oak Leaves was awarded to General Johann David Ludwig von Yorck for his leadership in the Army.

During the First World War the *Orden Pour le Mérite* with Oak Leaves was Germany's highest award for individual gallantry in action. Not one was awarded to any member of the German Army Air Service. Of the award *Pour le Mérite*, 81 of these awards were made to German Aviation personnel during the First World War. The Order was discontinued after the defeat of Germany in 1918.

It is considered by some that the colloquial name 'Blue Max', which was introduced during the First World War, was derived from the Order's physical description which in essence was a blue Maltese cross. The Germans pronounce the word Maltese as 'Maaltese'; if this word is then corrupted to 'Maa' and the word 'cross' is replaced by an 'X', then the term 'Blue Max' can be derived. There is also a school of thought that the award was named the 'Blue Max' after the death of its first military aviation recipient – Max Immelmann.

The famous Iron Cross was instituted by Friedrich Wilhelm III, King of Prussia, in 1813 as an award for gallantry in combat. It had two classes (1st and 2nd) plus a Grand Cross, but the latter was only awarded 19 times up to 1918. A special category, the Grand Cross on a Star, was created and awarded to Field Marshal Blücher after the Battle of Waterloo and to Field Marshal von Hindenburg in 1918.

*Prussian Military Merit Cross in Gold, awarded to NCOs for bravery. It was regarded as the equivalent to the Pour le Mérite for officers.*

The 1st and 2nd Classes of the Iron Cross were reinstated for the Franco-German War of 1870–71 and continued to be awarded until the end of the First World War. There were 219,300 awards made of the Iron Cross 1st Class and 5,500,000 of the Iron Cross 2nd Class from 1813 to 1918. The Cross consisted of a cross patée in black iron edged with silver with a spray of oak leaves in the centre. The Imperial Crown and Royal Cypher were on the upper limb and the dates '1813', '1870', or '1914' respectively on the lower limb. The Iron Cross 1st Class was fixed to the uniform jacket like the Star of an Order, whereas the 2nd Class award was worn on the left breast from a black ribbon with white edges.

With the defeat of Germany in November 1918, the award of the Iron Cross was discontinued but on 2 September 1939 it was reinstated by Hitler as an Order with eight Divisions.

The Imperial German Aviation Service was regarded until 1916 as part of ground communications troops, although a separate command had been established in March 1915 but had not been unified. Naval and military aviation remained separate. At first, aviation units were controlled by the individual armies to which they were attached. For example Württemberg insisted that its aviation units were to be staffed only with its nationals. Politics and local pride created confusion.

This confused situation reigned until 8 October 1916, when General Ernst von Hoeppner was appointed Officer Commanding the Imperial German Aviation Service and immediately began to reorganise its structure, which resulted in there being fighter units of 18 aircraft each; ground attack units of six to twelve aircraft; bomber units with about 24 aircraft each; reconnaissance units; artillery units and single-seater aircraft for home defence. The Imperial German Naval Aviation Service however remained independent, operating flying boats from some 32 bases on the German and occupied coasts; they also operated land-based aircraft for coastal defences.

In Germany there was a certain social attitude towards flying aircraft in the early years. Prior to 1914 gentlemen of means employed chauffeurs to drive their cars and the piloting of an aircraft was regarded in the same manner.

The first pilots were drawn from the ranks of non-commissioned officers, while the commissioned officers – usually cavalrymen, some with the rank Freiherr (Baron) – acted as observers and sat in the rear cockpit. This sometimes caused great problems, as in the early years most of the 'cavalrymen' insisted on being properly dressed and that included the wearing of a sword. As the aircraft were made of wood and fabric, this caused holes to be torn in the fuselage areas and the practice of carrying a sword was very soon dropped. However, it was not long before these frustrated cavalrymen were drawn into the excitement of the chase and quickly grasped the knightly chance of individual combat in the air – of flying out to offer, symbolically, the single tilting of the lance at their enemies as the knights of medieval times had done.

With the onset of the First World War the pilots soon became household names and the German High Command had photographs taken of these 'Knights of the Air'. These photographs were in postcard style and were called Sanke cards. They were enthusiastically collected, giving the pilots a kind of film-star status and ensuring that they would be fêted wherever they went. But behind this facade lay the grim truth of war, and the vast majority of these young knights died before they could even enjoy their new-found fame. This book is about some of those men, the holders of the award *Orden Pour le Mérite*.

# General Introduction

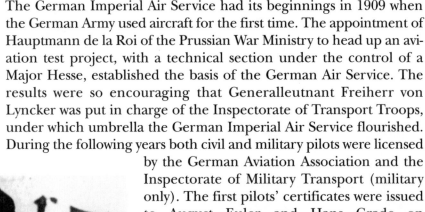

The German Imperial Air Service had its beginnings in 1909 when the German Army used aircraft for the first time. The appointment of Hauptmann de la Roi of the Prussian War Ministry to head up an aviation test project, with a technical section under the control of a Major Hesse, established the basis of the German Air Service. The results were so encouraging that Generalleutnant Freiherr von Lyncker was put in charge of the Inspectorate of Transport Troops, under which umbrella the German Imperial Air Service flourished. During the following years both civil and military pilots were licensed by the German Aviation Association and the Inspectorate of Military Transport (military only). The first pilots' certificates were issued to August Euler and Hans Grade on 1 February 1910. Euler – an engineer – went on to become an aircraft designer. During the spring of 1910 the first flying schools were set up, and by the December of that year, ten officers had completed their flying training and had been awarded their certificates.

*Hans Grade who, together with August Euler, was awarded pilot's certificate No. 2, 1910.*

The German War Department, encouraged by the results of military pilot training, allocated the sum of 110,000 marks for the purchase of military aircraft. The future Imperial German Air Service was slowly coming into being and when the First World War broke out on 4 August 1914, Germany had 228

aircraft on its strength, plus a small reserve. Aircrew strength stood at 600 officer pilots and 220 NCO pilots; 500 officers had qualified as observers – a total of 1,320 flying personnel. This complement was allocated to 41 *Flieger Abteilungs* (Flying Units) of which 33 were *Feldflieger Abteilungs* (Field Aviation Units). Eight *Abteilungs* were designated *Fortress Flieger Abteilungs,* whose role was to defend strategic towns.

German Army aircraft were placed under the control of the military whilst their large fleet of airships was placed under the control of the Navy. At this time German thinking was that aircraft and airships were to be used for reconnaissance – aircraft for short-range missions, such as artillery spotting and photo-reconnaissance, and airships for long-range reconnaissance duties. The tactical use of aircraft as fighters and bombers was to come shortly.

The first long-range bomber units – *Kampfgeschwader* (KG) – were formed in October 1914 and came under army command. The first such unit was a clandestine one codenamed *Brieftauben Abteilung* Ostend (BAO) Ostend Carrier Pigeon Flight, under the command of Major Wilhelm Siegert.

The German High Command soon realised that their relatively slow reconnaissance and observation aircraft needed protection from faster enemy fighters, so that they could carry out their essential missions unmolested. Early German fighters – such as the Aviatik C1 – were two-seaters with the pilot and observer firing machine-guns sidewards and rearwards from their cockpits. The aircrew were

*Gotha bombers being loaded with bombs.*

unable to fire forward through the propeller arc as no firing interrupter gear had yet been perfected. Some aircraft had machine-guns mounted on the upper wing to fire over the propeller arc but this was not very successful.

It was not long before a reliable firing interrupter mechanism was developed. The mechanism was said to have been invented by Anthony Fokker after seeing the French pilot Roland Garros's design on his Morane Parasol, after it had been shot down. (It is now accepted that it was probably the brainchild of Heinrich Luebbe, a member of Fokker's design team.) On 23 May 1915 his Fokker Eindecker – equipped with a machine-gun firing through the propeller – came into front-line service with FA62 at Douai. German

*German Gothas in front of airship hangar at Gontrode.*

Air Service fighter aircraft now came into their own: single-seaters with machine-guns firing forward through the propeller.

This development attracted the attention of Hauptmann Oswald Boelcke and Oberleutnant Max Immelmann – both already famous in Germany as pilots. Boelcke and Immelmann immediately went into combat with the new Eindeckers of FA62. Boelcke shot down a Morane Parasol on 4 July and Immelmann a BE2c on 1 August 1915. Both were soon to earn Imperial Germany's highest decoration – the *Pour le Mérite* – on 12 January 1916.

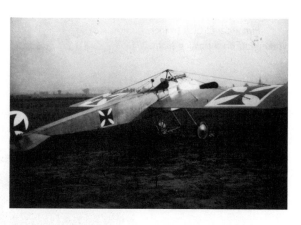

*Fokker E.I Scout with its forward-firing machine-gun. N.B. Note headrest for pilot to ensure correct sighting.*

With the arrival of the Eindeckers with their forward-firing guns, the German Air Service attained air superiority over the Allied air services, until the Allies produced their own aircraft with forward-firing machine-guns.

The aerial experience of war began to show that the German Imperial Air Service needed some central command structure. The War Ministry approved a unified aviation command in 1915 and appointed Major Hermann von der Leith-Thomsen as Chief of Field Aviation, with a brief to reorganise the Service. By the summer of 1915 the German Air Service had been expanded to 80 *Abteilungs*. The BAO bomber unit was enlarged to six squadrons of six aircraft each and another separate unit – *Brieftauben Abteilung* Metz – was formed at Metz.

Recognising the need for specific fighter-pilot training, *Kampfeinsitzer* (single-seat fighter) *Abteilung* Nr.1 was formed at Mannheim on 1 August 1915. All of the trainees were already qualified two-seater aircraft pilots. When trained, these fighter pilots would fly and protect the vital two-seaters engaged in artillery spotting and reconnaissance missions. Major Leith-Thomsen rapidly improved the Air Service and in autumn 1916 was appointed Chief of the General Staff to the Commanding General of the Air Service, Generalleutnant Ernst von Hoeppner.

Shrewdly, the German War Ministry realised the propaganda value of casting their pilots and observers as national heroes, by awarding honours and decorations for the number of enemy aircraft shot down. At first four victories were needed to give 'ace' status, although the Germans did not use this term, preferring the term '*Kanone*' (cannon). Six kills were rewarded with the award of the Knight's Cross of the Hohenzollern House Order and eight for the award of

*Halberstadt CL.II trainer taking off on a training flight.*

the *Pour le Mérite*. The famous 'Teutonic Knights of the Air' began to emerge: Boelcke, Immelmann and Wintgens won the 'Blue Max' for their exploits and were immortalised on the famous Sanke cards. These postcards carried the portraits of the aerial knights in various heroic poses and were avidly bought and collected by an admiring German public.

During the winter of 1916 the tempo of aerial conflict increased and the number of victories required for high honours increased. To gain the *Pour le Mérite*, 16 kills were needed, which later rose to 20 and by the end of the war, 30. Strangely, some pilots with high scores – including Leutnant Paul Billik with 31 kills and Josef Mai with 30 kills – were never awarded the Blue Max. Thirty-five other pilots scored between 14 and 26 victories but were not decorated with the *Pour le Mérite*.

Nineteen known pilots were actually awarded the decoration but never received it for various reasons, including death. The decoration could only be awarded to a living officer. Non-commissioned ranks received the Golden Military Service Cross, of which there were 80 awards.

*German fighter pilot Josef Mai, who despite having scored 30 victories was never awarded the* Pour le Mérite.

During the Battle of the Somme the Allies regained air superiority so in August 1916 the German Air Service Command formed permanent fighter squadrons equipped with the new D-type aircraft coming into service. These squadrons – *Jagdstaffel* (hunting or fighter squadrons) – soon became known as *Jastas*. Their primary function was to hunt, attack and destroy enemy fighters (and other aircraft and balloons) so that German artillery spotting and reconnaissance aircraft could carry out their duties unhindered. This fixed fighter role was to prove successful.

The new Albatros D.I and D.II scouts were in service and could outfly most of the aircraft of the Allied Air Services, which were handicapped by the lack of an aircraft which could outperform the formidable Albatros. The British Pup and the French Nieuport were the best the Allies could put in the air. By the end of 1916 the German Air Service had 24 fully staffed operational *Jastas* and these began to take an even higher toll of Allied aircraft. Many fighter pilots began to rise to prominence, including Hartmut Baldamus, Erwin

*Albatros D.II belonging to Leutnant Max Böhme of Jasta 5. Seen here being examined by members of the British RFC after it was shot down.*

Böhme, Otto Bernert, Albert Dossenbach, Wilhelm Frankl, Heinrich Gontermann, Max Müller, Hans Müller and Werner Voss. Fate, however, took a hand and the famous Hauptmann Oswald Boelcke died in combat with DH.2s of 24 Squadron, RFC, on 28 October 1916, his aircraft colliding with one of his former flying pupils, Erwin Böhme.

Boelcke's death brought to the fore the most famous of all German aces – Freiherr Manfred von Richthofen. By the end of 1916 he had 15 confirmed victories to his credit. In January 1917 von Richthofen took command of *Jasta* 11 and, under his inspired leadership, it became the second highest scoring *Jasta* in the German Air Service. During April 1917 – known to the Allies as 'Bloody April' – Richthofen's *Jasta* 11 shot down 89 enemy aircraft with their Albatros D.IIIs. Richthofen had his Albatros painted bright red, which gained him his nickname the 'Red Baron'.

*Nieuport 10.*

*Wreckage of DH.2 No. 5994 of No. 29 Squadron, flown by Lieutenant K K Turner, being examined by German soldiers.*

*Sopwith Camels of No. 8(N) Squadron lined up at Mont St Eloi Airfield, Christmas 1917.*

More and more fighter pilots rose to national (and international) fame: Karl Allmenröder, Lothar von Richthofen (brother of the Red Baron), Karl Schäfer, Adolf von Tutschek and Kurt Wolff. The German Air Service, though outnumbered, now had air superiority over the Allies, with the RFC taking heavy casualties. To counteract their numerical inferiority, the *Jastas* were combined into groups – *Jagdgeschwader* (JG). *Jastas* 4, 6, 10 and 11 were combined as JG Nr.1 under the command of Manfred von Richthofen. Being highly

mobile, JG 1 soon became known as the 'Flying Circus' because of its ability to move quickly from battlefront to battlefront.

By the summer of 1917 the RFC – reinforced with Sopwith Triplanes of the RNAS – had regained control of the air. New aircraft, such as the Bristol F2b, the Sopwith Camel, and the famous SE5 were coming into front-line service and restored the balance. The French Air Service Squadrons of Spad V.II and Spad X.IIIs were also coming into service and gained many successes.

The Allies' objective was to overwhelm the German Air Service in the air by numerical superiority, but the Allied pilots, to a certain extent, were not such skilled airmen as the Germans at this time. However, the RFC was soon to change this and gain the edge. Tactical bombing by DH.4s and then DH.9 day bombers was increased. Fighting back, the German Air Service took delivery of the Albatros D.V and the Pfalz D.VIII, but these fighters made little impact, in spite of the superior flying skills of the German pilots.

The Fokker Dr.I Triplane (*Dreidecker*) came into service in the autumn of 1917 but had to be withdrawn due to problems with its wings. It re-entered service later and Kurt Wolff was killed in action flying the new Triplane on 15 September. The high scoring Werner Voss, also flying a Triplane, fell in action against SE5s of the élite 56 Squadron, RFC. Another ace, Heinrich Gonterman, destroyer of 17 observation balloons, was killed when his Triplane's top wing folded in flight.

The German Knights of the Air continued to die in combat. Karl Schäfer, Eduard Ritter von Dostler and Erwin Böhme fell, and the Red Baron himself was wounded and hospitalised. New knights appeared in the sky; Fritz Rumey and Otto Konnecke of *Jasta* 5 took up the mantle and many Allied aircraft fell beneath their guns.

*Fokker Dr.I Triplane flown by Leutnant von Linsingen of Jasta 11 being prepared for a flight.*

As 1918 arrived, famous names continued to fall in aerial combat. Walter von Bülow died on 4 January and Max Ritter von Müller on 9 January under the guns of the RFC. The brave Müller jumped to his death from his blazing aircraft, preferring a quick death rather the agony of death by fire.

January 1918 also saw the Fokker Triplane come into its own when von Richthofen discovered the agility of the machine in a dogfight. Again he had his aircraft painted in bright red. Whole *Jastas* were equipped with the Triplanes, others partly equipped. The Triplanes of von Richthofen's 'Flying Circus' scored the most victories during March and April 1918. The seemingly invincible Red Baron met his inevitable end on 21 April 1918, shot down in action by Australian ground forces on the Somme.

With the United States of America now in the war, the German Government realised that they would have to increase their air arm to compete with America's industrial might. Accordingly the 'Amerika Programm' was instituted to increase production of aircraft. Forty new *Jastas* were created and two new *Jagdgeschwaders*. Hauptmann Adolf von Tutschek commanded JG.II and Oberleutnant Bruno Loerzer JG.III. Aircrew reinforcements became available from the now defunct Russian Front – these pilots and observers were battle-hardened from flying in Russia and provided a valuable pool of new blood.

Other pilots began to show their worth: Oberleutnant Ernst Udet – who ended the war with 62 victories and was the highest surviving ace – was posted to *Jasta* 11. Oberleutnant Hermann Wilhelm Göring – later to become Reichsmarschall in Nazi Germany – was appointed to command von Richthofen's JG1, but only scored one

*Aircraft of the United States Air Service (USAS) at Main Field at Issoudon.*

*Fokker D.VIIs of JG.3 at Nivelles, December 1918.*

more kill to bring his total to 22 victories. During April 1918 JG 1 began to receive one of Germany's best fighters of the First World War – the Fokker D.VII. This aircraft went on to become Germany's outstanding fighter of the war.

By the end of May most of the German Air Service was battling against the French and United States Air Services on the Aisne front. The RFC had established air superiority over the British section of the front and was flying sorties without opposition over and behind the German lines. The Allies' war of attrition had begun to tell and the German Air Service began to run out of experienced aircrew. The last of the Knights of the Air took to the sky in the summer of 1918, flying their Fokker D.VIIs into combat.

The German Imperial Air Service was fighting on other fronts – Palestine, Italy and the Dardanelles – where Hauptmann Hans Buddecke had gained the third *Pour le Mérite* of the war on 14 April 1916.

*Lloyd C.V two-seat reconnaissance aircraft of Austro-Hungarian FLIK 30, 1917.*

In Italy the German Air Service had been assisting their allies, the Austro-Hungarians, with three *Jastas*. With the big German offensives in France, these *Jastas* were withdrawn and the Austro-Hungarians fought on unaided.

The German Imperial Naval Air Service, with their own seaplane fighters and land-based aircraft, duelled with their British counterparts over the North Sea. Oberleutnant Friedrich Christiansen won his *Pour le Mérite* on 11 December 1917. His exploits included

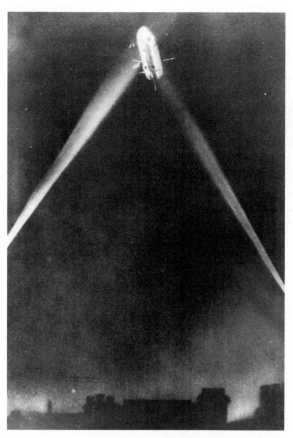

*German Zeppelin caught in the searchlights over London during a raid.*

an air-to-surface battle against a British submarine, the C.25, at the mouth of the River Thames. Two other naval fliers, Oberleutnant Gotthard Sachsenberg and Leutnant Theo Osterkamp, scored many kills and both were awarded the *Pour le Mérite*.

The German Naval Airship Division, flying Zeppelins, made many raids over England. Kapitänleutnant Horst Treusch Freiherr von Buttlar-Brandenfels won his *Pour le Mérite* for completing 19 missions against England, and Fregatten Kaptain Peter Strasser won the supreme award in 1917, but lost his life in Zeppelin L70 when leading a mass Zeppelin attack against England. The last three months of the war saw the German Air Service still hard at battle. On 8 August 1918 the RAF suffered its highest number of casualties of the First World War with its pilots being shot down by aces Otto Konnecke, Erich Löwenhardt, Lothar von Richthofen, Ernst Udet and Arthur Laumann.

The ground war, however, was going badly for the Germans, but their Air Service, though hard pressed and outnumbered three to one, was still an effective fighting force. During September 1918 they inflicted the most aerial casualties sustained by the Allies since April 1917.

At 11 a.m. on 11 November 1918 the First World War ended and the Germans capitulated. The German Air Service was bruised, battered, bloodied but unbowed. Their aircraft were broken up and smashed into a thousand pieces, such was the legacy they left behind. They had fought the good fight, largely with honour, but had succumbed to the overwhelming material power and resources of the Allies. Some, but not many, of the Teutonic Knights of the Air survived the First World War, only to die between the wars through murder, revolution or by accident, although a few did serve again in the Second World War for their fatherland, Nazi Germany – but then that is another story.

# Holders of the *Ordern Pour le Mérite*

† Allmenröder, Leutnant Karl
(1896–1917)

Althaus, Oberleutnant Ernst Freiherr
von (1890–1946)

Baümer, Leutnant Paul
(1896–1927)

† Beaulieu-Marconnay, Leutnant Oliver
Freiherr von (1898–1918)

† Bernert, Oberleutnant Fritz Otto
(1893–1918)

† Berr, Oberleutnant Hans
(1890–1917)

Berthold, Hauptmann Rudolf
(1891–1920)

Blume, Leutnant Walter
(1896–1964)

† Boelcke, Hauptmann Oswald
(1891–1916)

Boenigk, Oberleutnant Oskar
Freiherr von (1893–1946)

† Böhme, Leutnant der Reserve Erwin
(1879–1917)

Bolle, Rittmeister Karl (1893–1955)

Bongartz, Leutnant der Reserve
Heinrich (1892–1946)

Brandenburg, Hauptmann Ernst von
(1883–1952)

Büchner, Leutnant Franz
(1898–1920)

Buckler, Leutnant der Reserve Julius
(1894–1960)

† Buddecke, Hauptmann Hans-Joachim
(1890–1918)

† Bülow-Bothkamp, Leutnant Walter
von (1894–1918)

Buttlar-Brandenfels, Kapitänleutnant
Horst Freiherr Treusch von
(1888–1943)

Christiansen, Kapitänleutnant zur See
Friedrich (1879–1972)

Degelow, Leutnant Carl
(1891–1970)

† Dossenbach, Leutnant der Reserve
Albert (1891–1917)

† Dostler, Oberleutnant Eduard Ritter
von (1892–1917)

† Frankl, Leutnant der Reserve
Wilhelm (1893–1917)

Fricke, Oberleutnant Hermann
(1890–?)

† Gontermann, Leutnant der Reserve
Heinrich (1896–1917)

Göring, Oberleutnant Hermann
Wilhelm (1893–1946)

Greim, Oberleutnant Robert Ritter
von (1892–1945)

Griebsch, Leutnant der Reserve
Wilhelm (1887–1920)

Grone, Oberleutnant Jürgen von
(1887– ?)

Hoeppner, General der Kavallerie
Ernst von (1860–1922)

**Legend**

Freiherr von = Baron of.
Hereditary title granted by
Royal decree to the family.

Ritter von = Knight of.
Title of noblity granted as a
Royal reward for services
rendered.

† = Killed in action.

† Höhndorf, Leutnant Walter
(1892–1917)

Homburg, Oberleutnant Erich
(1886–?)

Horn, Oberleutnant Hans-Georg
(1892–?)

† Immelmann, Oberleutnant Max
(1890–1916)

Jacobs, Leutnant Josef Carl Peter
(1894–1978)

Keller, Hauptmann Alfred
(1882–1974)

† Kirschstein, Leutnant Hans
(1896–1918)

Kissenberth, Oberleutnant Otto
(1893–1919)

Klein, Oberleutnant der Reserve
Hans (1891–1944)

† Kleine, Kapitänleutnant Rudolf
(1886–1917)

Köhl, Hauptmann Hermann
(1888–1938)

Könnecke, Leutnant Otto
(1892–1956)

Kroll, Oberleutnant Heinrich
Claudius (1894–1930)

Laumann, Leutnant der Reserve
Arthur (1894–1970)

† Leffers, Leutnant der Reserve Gustav
(1892–1916)

Leith-Thomsen, Oberst Hermann von
der (1867–1942)

Leonhardy, Hauptmann Leo
(1880–1928)

Loerzer, Hauptmann Bruno
(1891–1960)

† Löwenhardt, Oberleutnant Erich
(1897–1918)

Menckhoff, Hauptmann Karl
(1883–1948)

† Müller, Leutnant Max Ritter von
(1887–1918)

Müller-Kahle, Oberleutnant Albert
(1894–?)

† Mulzer, Leutnant Max Ritter von
(1893–1916)

Neckel, Leutnant Ulrich (1898–1928)

Nielebock, Leutnant der Landwehr
Friedrich (1882–?)

Osterkamp, Oberleutnant zur See
Theodor (1892–1975)

† Parschau, Leutnant Otto
(1890–1916)

Pechmann, Oberleutnant Paul
Freiherr von (1889–?)

† Pütter, Leutnant Fritz
(1895–1918)

Richthofen, Oberleutnant Lothar
Freiherr von (1894–1922)

† Richthofen, Rittmeister Manfred
Freiherr von (1892–1918)

Rieper, Leutnant der Reserve Peter
(1887–?)

† Röth, Oberleutnant Friedrich Ritter
von (1893–1918)

† Rumey, Leutnant der Reserve Fritz
(1891–1918)

Sachsenberg, Oberleutnant zur See
Gotthard (1891–1961)

† Schäfer, Leutnant Karl Emil
(1891–1917)

Schleich, Hauptmann Eduard Ritter
von (1888–1945)

† Schreiber, Leutnant Wilhelm Paul
(?–1918)

† Strasser, Fregattenkapitän Peter
(1876–1918)

Thom, Leutnant Karl (1893–?)

Thuy, Leutnant Emil (1894–1930)

† Tutschek, Hauptmann Adolf Ritter
von (1891–1918)

Udet, Oberleutnant Ernst
(1896–1941)

Veltjens, Leutnant der Reserve Joseph
(1894–1943)

† Voss, Leutnant der Reserve Werner
(1897–1917)

Walz, Hauptmann Franz
(1885–1945)

† Windisch, Leutnant der Reserve
Rudolf (1897–1918?)

† Wintgens, Leutnant Kurt
(1894–1916)

† Wolff, Oberleutnant der Reserve Kurt
(1895–1917)

Wüsthoff, Leutnant der Reserve Kurt
(1897–1926)

# Biographies of the Holders of the *Orden Pour le Mérite*

## Leutnant Karl ALLMENRÖDER
(1896–1917)

Karl Allmenröder was born on 3 May 1896 in the small town of Wald near Solingen. The son of a Lutheran Pastor, his strict upbringing and education were instrumental in his choosing to become a doctor, but his studies were interrupted by the outbreak of war. He enlisted in the German Army, joined Field Regiment 62 and after training was posted to the 20th Field Regiment, but within months he returned to the 62nd. He saw active service in Poland and was awarded the Iron Cross 2nd Class at the beginning of March 1915, which resulted in him being awarded a commission on 30 March, and at the beginning of August 1915 he was awarded the Friedrich August Cross 1st Class.

By this time his brother Willi had enlisted in the German Army and together they applied, and were accepted, for the German Army Air Service on 29 March 1916. On completion of their flying training at the Flying School at Halberstadt, they were both posted to FA 227 and in November 1916 to *Jasta* 11 (Royal Prussian). *Jasta* 11 was led by the already legendary Manfred von Richthofen and was destined to become the second highest scoring *Jasta* in the German Air Service.

Karl Allmenröder scored his first victory on 16 February 1917 when he shot down a BE2c of 16 Squadron, RFC. By the end of March he had raised his tally to four and had been awarded the Iron Cross 1st Class. April started well with a victory over a BE2 of 13 Squadron, RFC, over Lens. On 25, 26 and 27 April he shot down three aircraft on consecutive days, bringing his tally to eight. This

*Portrait of Leutnant Karl Allmenröder wearing his Pour le Mérite. On his left breast can be seen in descending order: Iron Cross 1st Class, Friedrich August Cross 1st Class and his pilot's badge.*

*Willi Allmenröder with his pilot in their Albatros B.II.*

success was marred by the news that his brother Willi, who had scored two victories, had been severely wounded in a dogfight and invalided out of the German Army Air Service.

In May, 13 victories brought Karl Allmenröder's tally to 21. June saw his relentless pursuit of the enemy bring his tally to 25. On 6 June, he was awarded the Knight's Cross of the Hohenzollern House Order and the following day the coveted *Pour le Mérite* (Blue Max). Although June was to start dramatically well for Karl Allmenröder, it was to end tragically. On 18, 24, 25 and 26 June, four more British aircraft were shot down by him, bringing his tally to 29. Then at 9.45 a.m. on 27 June his patrol was attacked by British fighters over Zillebeke and his plane crashed, killing him instantly. He was posthumously awarded the Oldenburg Friedrich August Cross 1st and 2nd Class and the Bayern *Militar Kronen* Order 4th Class on 20 July 1917. He was just 21 years old.

### Oberleutnant der Reserve Ernst Freiherr von ALTHAUS (1890–1946)

The son of the Adjutant to the Duke of Saxe-Coburg-Gotha, Ernst Althaus was born on 19 March 1890 at Coburg, Bavaria. At the age of 16 he joined the 1st Royal Saxon Hussar Regiment of the Royal

Saxon Army Corps as an ensign, being promoted to Leutnant in 1911.

Three years later the war broke out and the 1st Royal Saxon Hussars were immediately into action. On 27 January 1915 he was awarded the Saxon Knight's Cross to the Order of St Heinrich and the Iron Cross 2nd Class, for his bravery in a number of clashes with the enemy. But his sights were set on joining the German Air Service and on 4 April 1915 he was transferred; on completion of his training he was promoted to Oberleutnant and became known as 'Hussar Althaus'. It is a fact that a number of the Hussars who transferred to the German Air Service used to wear their sabres when flying, often damaging the fabric of the aircraft when climbing in and out. It was a practice that soon ceased.

Ernst Freiherr von Althaus was posted to FA23 on 20 September and from there to various *Kampf Kommandos* – *Kek* Vaux (this unit later became part of *Jasta* 4), Jamitz and Sivry. He recorded his first victory on 3 December 1915 when he shot down a BE2c of 13 Squadron whilst flying west of Roye. His next victory was a French Voisin belonging to *Escadrille* VB101 on 2 February 1916, followed by another BE2c on 26 February. On 19 March he raised his tally to four when he shot down a Caudron GIV, followed by a Farman on 30 April whilst on patrol over St Mihiel. At the end of April 1916, having increased his score to five, he was wounded in the leg during a dog-fight. Althaus was taken to hospital for treatment and it was there that he met a nurse who was later to be his wife. He returned to his unit after convalescence, to be told that he had been awarded the Iron

*Oberleutnant Ernst Freiherr von Althaus standing beside his Fokker Eindecker. N.B. note the headrest.*

Cross 1st Class and the Knight's Cross with Swords of the Hohenzollern House Order. This was followed in July 1916 by the coveted award, the *Pour le Mérite*. Von Althaus continued to fly with his unit until 4 March 1917 when he was again wounded in combat. During the time he was in hospital, *Kek* Vaux became *Jasta* 4. By this time his tally was nine.

After a period of recuperation he was posted to *Jasta* 14, but shortly afterwards was picked by Manfred von Richthofen to take command of *Jasta* 10. Whilst with *Jasta* 10 he flew Albatros D.V No.D1119/17 with his nickname 'HA' (Hussar Althaus) painted in morse code – five dots and one dash – on the side. His last confirmed victory was on 24 July 1917 when he shot down Sopwith Camel B3825 of 70 Squadron, RFC. One month later he relinquished command of *Jasta* 10 to Werner Voss when his eyesight started to fail. He was given command of *Jastaschule* 11 for a time but his eyesight continued to worsen. He later returned to army duties where he commanded an infantry company in the Verdun area. He was captured by the US Army on 15 October 1918 and was imprisoned in a POW camp until the end of September 1919.

At the end of the war he entered the legal profession and became a barrister, but went blind in 1937. Despite his blindness he continued to study law and during the Second World War was appointed the Director of the County Court of Berlin. In 1945 he worked for a short time with the Allies as an interpreter, but died after a short illness on 29 November 1946. His list of decorations was extremely impressive and in addition to the *Pour le Mérite* and the Knight's Cross with Swords of the Hohenzollern House Order, he held the Sax-Ernestine House Order, Knight 2nd Class with Swords, the Brunswick War Merit Cross 2nd Class and the Hesse Honour Decoration for Bravery.

## Leutnant Paul BAÜMER
(1896–1927)

Paul Baümer was born on 11 May 1896 at Duisberg and spent most of his childhood fascinated by the giant Zeppelins that operated from Friedrichshafen near his home, spending every second he could watching them. On leaving school he found himself a job as a dental assistant and among the dentist's patients was a pilot who persuaded him that he ought to take up flying. He joined the local flying club, paying for his own lessons. His first flight had a rather ignominious end to it as he landed in a tree whilst trying to land. However he persevered, finally obtaining his licence. When the war broke out, Paul Baümer tried to enlist as a naval airman, but was turned down. The reason is not known. He then volunteered for the 70th Infantry Regiment at Saarbrücken and after training saw combat at St Quentin in France. In the early part of 1915 he was posted to the XXI Army Corps on the Russian Front where he was badly wounded in the left arm.

Whilst recovering in hospital he applied for transfer to the German Air Service, but again was refused. He then heard about vacancies in the German Air Service for technicians and using his experience as a dental assistant, persuaded the authorities to accept his transfer. At the beginning of 1916 he was accepted for 'General Duties' in the German Air Service and posted to Döbritz. Within a few months he had persuaded the Commanding Officer to look at his previous flying experience and put his name forward for flying training. The spring of 1916 saw Paul Baümer at flying school and such was the ease with which he qualified that he was posted in October to *Armee Flugpark* No.1 as a ferry pilot and flight instructor. It was recognised that Baümer had a great deal to offer

*Pfalz D.VII.*

*Three-quarter portrait shot of Leutnant der Reserve Paul Baümer wearing the Pour le Mérite. The ribbon of the Golden Military Merit Cross, the Iron Cross 1st Class and Silver Wound Badge alongside his pilot's badge can also be seen on his tunic.*

and he was promoted on 19 February 1917 to the rank of Gefreiter, being posted to *Flieger Abteilung* 7 on 26 March. Three days later he was promoted again to Unteroffizier.

On 15 May, Paul Baümer was awarded the Iron Cross 2nd Class and within two days was sent for fighter training. On completion of his training he was posted to *Jasta* 2 (Boelcke) on 28 June for just two days, then on to *Jasta* 5. On 12, 13 and 15 July he scored his first three victories when he shot down three reconnaissance balloons, and for this he was awarded the Iron Cross 1st Class. Baümer was posted back to *Jasta* 2 in the August of 1917 and by the end of the year his tally had risen to 18.

On 12 February 1918, in recognition of his bravery, he was awarded the Gold Military Service Cross. His 19th victory, a Sopwith Camel shot down whilst on patrol over north Zonnebecke on 9 March, was recognised by granting him a commission in the rank of Leutnant on 10 April. The 200th victory of *Jasta* 2 (Boelcke) on 23 March was Baümer's 20th and was made even more remarkable by him shooting down two RE8 aircraft and one Camel in under three hours. Nine days later however, whilst trying to land a badly shot-up Pfalz D.VIII, Paul Baümer was injured in the crash-landing, breaking his jaw amongst other injuries. He returned to *Jasta* 2 in the September and was immediately given the nickname of 'Der Eiserne Adler' (The Iron Eagle) after being awarded the Silver Wound Badge. By the end of September he had increased his tally to 38, including shooting down eight Allied aircraft in less than a week. Luck was on his side at this time, when he became one of the few pilots of the First World War to escape from his burning aircraft by using a parachute. His 30th victory brought the nation's highest award, a recommendation for the *Pour le Mérite*, which was awarded to him on 2 November. This award made him only one of five recipients of the *Pour le Mérite* <u>and</u> the Golden Military Merit Cross.

When the war ended, Paul Baümer had taken his tally to 43 victories. He went to work for Blohm and Voss, the ship and aeroplane builders, at their factory in Hamburg, but he could not settle and

*Leutnant der Reserve Paul Baümer of Jasta Boelcke walking toward his Pfalz D.VIII fighter.*

returned to his studies to become a professional dentist. Baümer continued his interest in flying by taking part in aerobatic competitions, before starting his own aircraft company – Baümer Aero GmbH – in Hamburg. His designers were the Guether brothers who later became famous working with the Ernst Heinkel design team. On 15 July 1927 during an aerobatic display over Copenhagen, and whilst testing the Rohrbach Rofix fighter, an all metal-cantilever monoplane, the aircraft stalled at 2,000 feet and spun into the waters of the Öre Sound. His body was later recovered and interred at Ohesdorf, near Hamburg.

## Leutnant Oliver Freiherr von BEAULIEU-MARCONNAY
(1898–1918)

The son of an aristocratic Prussian Army officer, Oliver Beaulieu-Marconnay was born in Berlin on 14 September 1898. During his early childhood he was brought up at Hochschule in the typical military fashion of the day, so it was no surprise when at 17 he joined up as a cadet one year after the beginning of the First World War. He enlisted in his father's old regiment, the 4th Prussian Dragoon Regiment and was almost immediately in combat. By the July of 1916, after battles in the Rokitno Swamps, he had been awarded the Iron Cross 1st Class and been promoted to the rank of Leutnant.

The young Leutnant Beaulieu-Marconnay had been observing the rise of the German Air Service and saw that it offered him the chance of achieving every Teutonic Knight's ambition, one-to-one combat. He applied to be transferred out of the Army and into the Air Service. Early in the spring of 1917 he was accepted and sent to flying training school, graduating in the November. On 1 December 1917 he was posted first to *Jasta* 18 (Royal Prussian), then a few months later to *Jasta* 15 (Royal Prussian) under the command of Leutnant Joseph Veltjens.

Under the tutelage of Joseph Veltjens he progressed rapidly and on 28 May 1918, 'Bauli', as he became known, scored his first victory, an AR2 over Soissons. This was quickly followed on 6 June by two victories, a DH.4 from 27 Squadron, RFC, and an SE5a from 32 Squadron. By the end of June he had raised his tally to eight, shooting down three Sopwith Camels, an SE5A and a DH.4. On 9 August he increased his score to 10 in the space of 15 minutes, when he shot down a Sopwith Camel and a Spad 2. Then on 2 September he was given command of *Jasta* 19 (Royal Prussian),

*Leutnant Oliver Freiherr von Beaulieu-Marconnay with his Fokker D.VII. The insignia relate to his former cavalry unit.*

when he was just 19 years old. By the end of September he had increased his tally to 21, a remarkable achievement considering the responsibilities of command and his tender years.

Beaulieu-Marconnay continued to fly combat missions and in the first two weeks of October had raised his score to 25. Then on 10 October 1918, whilst flying his favourite aircraft, a Fokker DV. II with his personal insignia – '4D' (the 4th Dragoons) – painted on the side of the blue fuselage, fate caught up with him. During a combat mission, in which they were attacked by Allied aircraft, his aircraft was caught in the crossfire from one of his own squadron members and he was mortally wounded. He managed to land the aircraft and was rushed to hospital. When the authorities were told of his injuries, they awarded him the coveted *Pour le Mérite* and rushed through the Order. As he lay dying, he was informed that he had been awarded the decoration – the youngest recipient of the 'Blue Max' in the First World War at the age of 20 years. He succumbed to his injuries and died on 26 October 1918.

## Oberleutnant Fritz Otto BERNERT
(1893–1918)

The son of the Burgermeister of Ratibor in Upper Silesia, Fritz Bernert was born on 6 March 1893. After leaving school he joined the 173rd Infantry Regiment as a cadet, being commissioned as a Leutnant just after the outbreak of the First World War. His infantry regiment was one of those which were very soon in the thick of the action. Bernert was wounded in November and was awarded the Iron Cross 2nd Class for his part in the action in which he received his wound. By the end of 1914 Bernert had been twice wounded again, fortunately none of his wounds being too serious. But in December 1914, during particularly heavy close-quarter fighting, he received a bayonet wound in his left arm which severed the main nerve. He was deemed to be unfit for further military duties, but the smell of battle was in his nostrils and he applied to join the German Army Air Service as an observer.

How Fritz Bernert passed the medical examination for the Air Service is a mystery, but he did, and in February 1915 he was sent for training. After graduating he was posted to FFA 27 and for six months carried out reconnaissance and scouting missions. Then in the July of 1915, Bernert was posted to FFA 71. By this time he was looking

*Portrait of Oberleutnant Fritz Otto Bernert wearing his Iron Cross 1st and 2nd Class, his Knight's Cross with Swords of the House of Hohenzollern Order and Saxon Albert Order Knight 2nd Class with Swords. Just above his belt can be seen his pilot's badge.*

towards flying the aircraft himself and applied for pilot training. In the November his application was accepted and he was posted to *Jastaschule* for training. Again he was able to conceal the fact that he only had one arm that was fully operational and another that had very limited mobility. In addition to this he was only one of three *Jasta* pilots in the German Army Air Service known to wear glasses. On graduating at the end of March 1916, Bernert was assigned to *Kek* Vaux where on 17 April he opened his tally by shooting down a Nieuport fighter.

During the summer months of 1916, there appeared to be a lull in the action in Fritz Bernert's sector and in the late August he was posted to *Jasta* 4. On 6 September he scored his second victory when he shot down a Caudron whilst on patrol over Dompierre. Another victory, a Nieuport fighter over Allenes on 11 September, raised his tally to three. By the end of November Bernert had raised his score to seven, the last three all on 9 November – two DH.2s and an FE.8.

In the February of 1917, Bernert was posted to *Jasta* 2 and was awarded the Iron Cross 1st Class, the Saxon Albert Order, Knight 2nd Class with Swords and Knight's Cross with Swords of the Hohenzollern House Order. To celebrate, Bernert opened his score with his new *Jasta* by shooting down a Sopwith Camel whilst on patrol over Ecourt-Mory, thus bringing his tally to eight. A BE2d at the end of March seemed to set the scene for April, when on consecutive days starting on the 1st, Bernert scored four victories. He continued to score almost daily, then on 23 April he was awarded Germany's highest accolade, the *Pour le Mérite*. As if to salute this honour, the following day, 24 April, Bernert claimed five victories in the one day, three BE2es (all from 9 Squadron, RFC), a DH.4 and a Sopwith 1½-Strutter. On 1 May, Bernert was appointed *Staffelführer* to *Jasta* 6 with his tally standing at 24. Bernert added three more victories to his score by the end of May before taking command of *Jasta* 2 (Boelcke) on 9 June 1917.

He continued to fly but with no more successes and on 18 August was wounded once again. On his release from hospital in the November, he was deemed to be unfit for flying duties and was assigned to the office of the Inspector of the Flying Service with promotion to Oberleutnant. In the early September of 1918, Otto Bernert contracted influenza and died in hospital in his home town on 18 October.

# Oberleutnant Hans BERR
(1890–1917)

Hans Berr was born on 20 May 1890 in Braunschweig, the son of the President of the Braunschweig High Postal Administration. He wanted to be a soldier from his earliest years and as soon as he was of age he enrolled in the Army as a cadet. By the time he was 18 years of age he had been commissioned as an Infantry Leutnant in the 4th Madgeburg (Reserve) Regiment. When the First World War broke out in 1914, Berr was serving with the 7th Light Infantry (Reserve) Regiment and was soon in action on the Western Front. He was

*Portrait shot of Oberleutnant Hans Berr wearing his* Pour le Mérite, *relaxing in his chair at* Jasta 5 *with his pet dog.*

wounded in action on 6 September 1914, which resulted in his being awarded the Iron Cross 2nd Class. He continued to serve in the Infantry and was promoted Oberleutnant on 27 January 1915, but like so many other young German aristocrats, he wanted to leave infantry ground combat and take to the air to do battle in a more exciting and personal way.

He applied to join the German Army Air Service on 3 March 1915 and was trained as an observer. After several months flying reconnaissance missions on the Western Front, Berr applied for pilot training and was accepted. He was posted to the *Jastaschule* at Metz where he was trained to fly single-seat fighters. On graduation he was posted to *Kek* Avillers flying Fokker Eindeckers. This *Staffel* later became *Jasta* 5.

On 8 March 1916 he opened his tally of kills when he shot down a Nieuport of *Escadrille* MS 3 over the Verdun sector of the front. A week later he downed a Caudron, also over Verdun. With but two victories to his credit he was appointed to command *Jasta* 5 (Royal Prussian) on 21 August 1916, based at Bechamp near Verdun in the 5th Army area. With the appointment came the awards of the Bavarian Military Merit Order 4th Class with Swords and the Brunswick War Merit Cross. *Jasta* 5 had been the Avillers Fokker *Staffel* and was originally equipped with Fokker Eindeckers, then re-equipped with Albatros D.II Scouts and Halberstadt D.IIs.

On the morning of 7 October 1916, he shot down a Caudron over Combles, then a BE2b of 34 Squadron also over Combles. These two victories brought his total to four confirmed but between 20 October and 26 October 1916, he added three more aircraft, two FE2bs and a Morane Parasol, together with a balloon shot down. His total now stood at eight and recognition followed in the form of decorations from Imperial Germany and its various States in the form of the Hanseatic Cross from Hamburg and the Ruess War Merit Cross and Honour Cross 3rd Class with Swords. By the time he had scored his tenth and final victory on 3 November 1916 he had been awarded

*Hans Berr and fellow pilots from Jasta 5 at a party given for von Althaus on his award of the Pour le Mérite.*

the Iron Cross 1st Class, the Knight's Cross with Swords of the Hohenzollern House Order, the Bavarian Military Merit Order 4th Class with Swords, the Brunswick War Merit Cross, the Ruess War Merit Cross and Honour Cross 3rd Class with Swords, and the Hamburg Hanseatic Cross.

On 4 December 1916 he was awarded Germany's highest decoration, the *Pour le Mérite*. This was before the German High Command had altered the required victory total to qualify for the 'Blue Max' to 16 aircraft shot down and confirmed. Hans Berr, proud holder of the *Pour le Mérite*, continued to fly in combat but did not add to his total victories.

Taking off with his *Jasta* 5 on Good Friday 6 April 1917, they engaged in aerial combat with 57 Squadron, RFC. In the heat of battle Vizefeldwebel Paul Hoppe, a fellow *Jasta* 5 pilot, had just moved in behind a Vickers Gunbus when Berr came swooping in from the right-hand side and crashed into Hoppe. Eyewitnesses said there was a big dust cloud and the tangled remains of both aircraft, locked together, plunged toward the ground, killing both pilots instantly.

### Hauptmann Rudolf BERTHOLD
(1891–1920)

Rudolf Berthold was born at Ditterswind, near Bamberg, northern Bavaria, on 24 March 1891, the son of a Franconian forester. His early childhood was uneventful and in 1910 at the age of 19, he joined the Army and was assigned to the 3rd Brandenburg Infantry Regiment Nr.20. However, the humdrum life of a soldier at that time was not for Berthold, so he decided to learn to fly at one of the private flying clubs that were starting to spring up. After gaining his licence No.538 on 26 September 1913, he asked for a transfer to the newly formed German Army Air Service. At the outbreak of war in 1914, Berthold was posted for flying training as an observer on Halberstadt two-seaters with FFA 23. By the end of the year he had been awarded the Iron Cross 2nd Class for his part in a number of reconnaissance flights and promoted to Feldwebel.

In 1915 Berthold transferred to DFWs and carried out a large number of reconnaissance flights over enemy lines. He was awarded the Iron Cross 1st Class in the autumn of 1915 and subsequently asked for a transfer to a fighter *Jasta*. He was sent to *Jastaschule* in the December of 1915 and on graduating was posted to *Kek* Vaux, flying single-seater Fokkers. On 2 February 1916, Rudolf Berthold opened his tally by shooting down a Voisin whilst on patrol over Chaulnes. By the end of April his tally stood at five and he had been awarded the *Bayerischer Kriegsverdienst Orden* IV Class, the *Ritterkreuz* of the St Heinrich's Order and the Saxon Knight's Cross of the Military St Henry Order. Returning from a mission on 25 April he suffered severe injuries from crash-landing a Pfalz E.IV after a serious misjudgment. Berthold returned to his unit before his wounds had properly healed (demonstrating an impatience he was later to repeat) and was commissioned to Leutnant.

In August 1916 Berthold was given command of *Jasta* 4 after forming this from *Kek* Vaux. Then on 27 August came another

*Portrait of Hauptmann Rudolf Berthold wearing his* Pour le Mérite.

award, the prestigious Knight's Cross with Swords of the Hohenzollern House Order. On 14 October he handed the reigns of *Jasta* 4 over to Hans Buddecke before taking command of *Jasta* 14. Berthold then started to mould his pilots into a team, and it was not until 24 March 1917 that he was to increase his personal tally by shooting down a Farman from *Escadrille* F7. Then in May 1917 his patrol was attacked by an Allied patrol and he was shot down by a British fighter. His aircraft crashed within his own lines and he was pulled from the wreckage, sustaining a fractured skull, a broken

*Hauptmann Rudolf Berthold leaning against the fuselage of his Fokker D.VII with its distinctive winged emblem on its side.*

*Hauptmann Rudolf Berthold (extreme left) with ground crew members in front of his Fokker Eindecker Scout.*

nose, pelvis and thigh. After two months in hospital, Berthold again discharged himself and returned to *Jasta* 14. On 12 August he was given command of Jasta 18 and promotion to Oberleutnant. He celebrated this by shooting down a Spad on 21 August and raising his tally to 13. In the month of September he scored 14 victories, bringing his tally to 27. On 2 October he scored his 28th victory by shooting down a DH.4 from 57 Squadron, RFC, but on 10 October 1917, during a dogfight with a British patrol, his right upper arm was smashed by a bullet. Whilst in hospital he received Germany's highest award, the *Pour le Mérite*, and ten days later was promoted to Hauptmann. Once again he discharged himself early and returned to his *Jasta*.

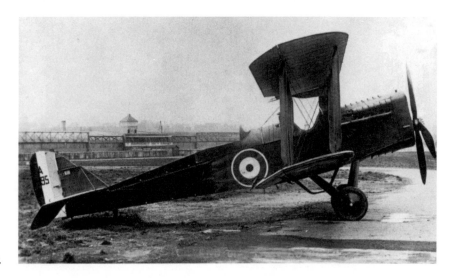

*De Havilland DH.4 bomber.*

Berthold was given command of *Jagdgeschwader* Nr.2 in March 1918, but he took with him nearly all the best pilots of *Jasta* 14, exchanging them with the pilots of *Jasta* 15 – not exactly an exercise in morale boosting for the men of *Jasta* 15! His aircraft, with his distinctive livery of a red and blue fuselage (red from the nose to the cockpit, then blue to the tail), with a winged sword painted on it, was one to be avoided by Allied pilots. On 10 August Berthold's patrol became involved with a patrol of DH.4s and during the ensuing dogfight, although Berthold shot down two of the Allied aircraft, he collided with the last one. His Fokker D.VII was badly damaged and Berthold struggled to keep it in the air, but in vain. It smashed into a house and although he survived the horrendous crash, it effectively ended his combat career.

On release from hospital, he found that the war was over, so in 1919 he joined the *Freikorps* and his unit, called the *Eiserne Schar* (Iron Horde), fought during the post-war revolution. On 15 March 1920 Berthold was in Harburg on the Elbe when he was attacked by rioters and it is said that he was beaten, then strangled with the ribbon of his *Pour le Mérite* – an ignominious end to such a respected Knight of the Air and one that was echoed by the inscription on his gravestone:

Honoured by his enemies – slain by his German brethren.

## Leutnant Walter BLUME
(1896–1964)

Walter Blume was born on 10 January 1896, in Hirschberg, a village at the foot of the Silesian mountains. After graduating from school in 1911, he took an apprenticeship as a toolmaker in a machine factory. At the outbreak of the First World War, he enlisted in the Silesian *Jäger* Battalion Nr.5 and was posted to East Prussia. The battalion had only been at the front a matter of months when, during heavy fighting near the town of Lyck, Blume was severely wounded. Whilst in hospital Blume considered his position and decided to apply for transfer, on his release, to the newly formed German Army Air Service.

On 30 June, with his application being approved, Blume reported to the Flying Reserve Unit at Grossenhain and was then posted to the Flying School at Leipzig-Mockau. On graduating and receiving his pilot's badge, Blume was assigned to the Research and Exercise Field

Unser erfolgreicher Kampfflieger
Leutnant Blume

*Leutnant Walter Blume in full flying kit standing in front of his Fokker D.VII.*

West Unit near St Quentin on the Western Front. After two months he was assigned to the Army Aeroplane Park A at Strassburg to await a posting to another unit. On 18 June 1916 Blume was assigned to *Feldflieger Abteilung* Nr.65 as a reconnaissance pilot, then one month later to FA(A) 280. Although being a reconnaissance pilot was not quite what Blume had in mind, he quickly distinguished himself and was awarded the Iron Cross 2nd Class on 24 July and promoted to Vizefeldwebel on 23 August 1916. Further flights during the rest of the year culminated in him being given a commission to Leutnant der Reserve on 31 January 1917.

At the beginning of March 1917, Blume was selected by Bruno Loerzer and Hermann Göring to be one of the pilots to form the nucleus of *Jasta* 26, a fighter unit. One month later, after conversion and tactical training, the squadron was ready and was assigned to the St Quentin area. Within days of arriving the *Jasta* was in action in some of the heaviest aerial fighting. On 10 May, Blume opened his tally when he shot down a DH.4 from 55 Squadron, RFC, whilst on patrol over Gouzeaucourt. He continued to score steadily and by the end of November had raised his score to six and had been awarded the Iron Cross 1st Class. Then on 29 November, during a patrol, his flight encountered some Bristol fighters from 48 Squadron, RFC, and during the skirmish Blume was hit in the chest. Managing to keep control of his aircraft, which had suffered considerable damage, and fighting waves of unconsciousness, Blume managed to guide his crippled aircraft back to his base. He had been critically wounded, but the skill of the surgeons and three months' hospitalisation aided his recovery.

On 5 March 1918, Blume returned to the front in command of *Jasta* 9 which was assigned to the Champagne Front. Within days Blume was in the skies and back with a vengeance. On 21 April he shot down a Spad whilst on patrol over Chiry-Ourscamps, taking his total of kills to seven. During the following three months he accounted for 10 more Allied aircraft, bringing his tally to 17. The

*Aerial shot of a Spad XIII.*

shooting down of a Spad over Bazoches on 6 August heralded the award of the Knight's Cross with Swords of the Hohenzollern House Order. By the end of September, Blume had raised his score to 26, followed on 2 October by his 28th victory and the *Jasta*'s 100th. On landing back at his field, Blume was ceremoniously awarded Germany's highest award, the *Pour le Mérite*. Blume scored his final victory on 28 October, a Sopwith Camel from 209 Squadron over Remaucourt, then came the Armistice and the end of the war.

Blume returned home to complete his engineering studies and earned a degree. He became a designer with the Arado and Albatros aviation companies and was responsible for contributing to many of the designs of aircraft used in the Second World War. Walter Blume died on 27 May 1964.

## Hauptmann Oswald BOELCKE
(1891–1916)

One of six children, Oswald Boelcke was born in Giebichenstein, near Halle in Saxony, on 19 May 1891. His father was a schoolteacher who ensured that all his children were educated to their full extent

*Hauptmann Oswald Boelcke standing at the entrance to the Headquarters of Jagdstaffel 2.*

and encouraged their enquiring minds. In Oswald Boelcke's case this was to manifest itself in later years, when he wrote his famous report on air fighting and tactics. After leaving school, Oswald Boelcke decided on a military career, much against the wishes of his family. In March 1911 he joined the Prussian Cadet Corps and was posted to No.3 *Telegrapher* Battalion at Koblenz. After completing his initial training, he was posted to the War School at Metz to finish his officer training.

After graduating, Boelcke applied for transfer to the German Army Air Service for training as a pilot and was accepted. He was posted to the flying school in Halberstadt, completing his flying training in October 1914. Boelcke was assigned to Trier in the first instance and two weeks later was posted to his first combat unit, FA 13, near Montmédy, where his older brother Wilhelm was stationed as an observer. The two brothers became a team, flying reconnaissance missions over the Argonne region. In October 1914, Boelcke received the Iron Cross 2nd Class for his work flying reconnaissance missions.

Boelcke continued flying reconnaissance missions into the first quarter of 1915 and received the Iron Cross 1st Class on 4 February. At the beginning of May, Boelcke was transferred to FA 62 which had recently been equipped with LVG C.1s. On 4 July 1915, with his observer Leutnant Heinz von Wuhlisch, Boelcke went on patrol over Valenciennes and encountered a Morane Parasol. After a short skirmish the Morane Parasol was shot down and Boelcke had opened his tally. His enthusiasm for engaging enemy aircraft whenever possible prompted the squadron commander to transfer Boelcke to single-seater fighters. The single-seat Fokker Eindeckers had recently been assigned to the squadron for scouting and protection of the reconnaissance aircraft. Early in the July, Boelcke saved the life of a 14-year-old French boy, for which he was awarded the Life Saving Medal. On 19 August, Boelcke, flying in a Fokker Eindecker from Douai, notched up

*Hauptmann Oswald Boelcke relaxing in the sunshine between sorties with an unknown member of his Jasta.*

his second victim when he shot down a Bristol biplane over the front lines. It was whilst at Douai that he came into contact with Max Immelmann, each one learning from the other. By the end of the year, Boelcke had raised his score to six and had been awarded the Knight's Cross with Swords of the Hohenzollern House Order.

In the first two weeks of January 1916, Boelcke shot down three more Allied aircraft bringing his total to nine and the was awarded Germany's highest award, the *Pour le Mérite.* He was the first fighter pilot to receive it. Every month, communiqués to the German High Command contained the name of Boelcke, as he steadily increased his tally. By the end of June 1916 it had reached 19 and Boelcke had become a household name in Germany. When Max Immelmann died in the June, the German High Command decided to send Boelcke on an inspection/public relations tour of Vienna, Budapest, Belgrade and Turkey. The long journeys gave him the chance to think of the way air fighting was progressing and he wrote a paper that he submitted to the German High Command, entitled 'Air Fighting Tactics'. It was to become the 'bible' amongst German fighter pilots in the following years.

At the end of July Boelcke was recalled from his tour and given command of *Jasta* 2 and promotion to Hauptmann. Boelcke decided to select some of his pilots and among those chosen were Manfred von Richthofen, Max Müller and Erwin Böhme. The latter was to play a significant part in Boelcke's demise later that year. On 2 September, Boelcke scored his 20th victory when he shot down a DH.2 from 37 Squadron, RFC. By the end of the month he had shot down nine more, bringing his tally to 29. *Jasta* 2 was creating a reputation for itself amongst the enemy as being one of the most feared in the German Army Air Service. The month of October was just as good for Boelcke in terms of victories and by 26 October he had shot down a further 11, bringing his total to 40.

Then on 28 October whilst on patrol with von Richthofen and Böhme, they came across seven enemy aircraft and dived to attack. Boelcke and Böhme, flying in tandem, chased a British fighter, then just as they were closing on it, another British fighter, chased by von Richthofen, cut across in front of them. Erwin Böhme rolled out of the way at the same time as Boelcke and the two aircraft collided. Böhme managed to control his aircraft, but Boelcke's Albatros D.II was badly damaged and spun toward the ground. The aircraft crashed behind a German gun emplacement where the crew pulled Boelcke from the wreckage. He had died almost immediately, no doubt because he never wore a helmet or a seat belt.

*The letter of condolence sent by the RFC together with a wreath at the death of German ace Oswald Boelcke*

## Oberleutnant Oskar Freiherr von BOENIGK
(1893–1946)

The son of an army officer, Oskar Boenigk was born in Siegersdorf, near Bunzlau, Silesia, on 25 August 1893. On leaving school, he followed the family tradition and became an army cadet. He was commissioned into the König Friedrich III Grenadier Regiment on 22 March 1912. By the time the First World War broke out, Boenigk was a platoon leader with his regiment and was soon in action. In October 1914, during the battle of Longwy, he was badly wounded in the chest and spent many months in hospital. For his part in the battle he was awarded the Iron Cross 2nd Class on his return to his unit in the early spring of 1915, and was soon in action again on the French Front where he was wounded again. He returned after recuperating and fought at Loretto Heights and Arras. Boenigk soon began to weary of the cold and the mud and looked toward the newly formed German Army Air Service. He applied for transfer to the Air Service, was accepted and was then posted to the observer school FEA 7 in December 1915 where, after training, he was posted to *Kampfstaffel* 19 of KG 4 in March 1916.

Boenigk spent the next four months on reconnaissance and scouting missions, then was posted to *Kampfstaffel* 32. At the beginning of January 1917 he applied to go to *Jastaschule* for training as a pilot and on graduating was posted to *Jasta* 4 on 24 June 1917. Boenigk opened

Unser ⟨erfolg⟩ ⟨reicher⟩ Kampfflieger
673    Oberleutnat. Freiherr von Boenigk

*Portrait of Oberleutnant Oskar Freiherr von Boenigk seen here wearing his Iron Cross 1st Class above his pilot's badge.*

his tally on 20 July, when he shot down a Sopwith Camel whilst on patrol over Tenbrielen. One week later he shot down another Sopwith Camel from 70 Squadron, RFC, whilst on patrol over Moorslede. By the end of September he had taken his score to five and was rewarded with the Iron Cross 1st Class and the command of *Jasta* 21 on 21 October. By the end of the year he had raised his tally to six.

The pressure of command and easing of hostilities meant that for the first six months of 1918 for Oskar Boenigk, things were very quiet. But at the beginning of June it all changed. Boenigk claimed six more victories – two Spads, one Breguet XIV and three balloons – bringing his total to 12. By the end of August he had increased it to 19 and had been awarded the Knight's Cross with Swords of the Hohenzollern House Order. He was also given command of JG 2 on 31 August and promoted to Oberleutnant. The *Geschwader* was moved to the St Mihiel Front in September to oppose the American forces that were massing there, and by the end of the month Boenigk had raised his personal tally to 26. At the beginning of October Boenigk received the Saxon Albert Order 2nd Class with Swords, the Sax-Ernestine House Order, Knight 2nd Class with Swords and the Prussian Order of St John, Knight of Honour. It was this last award that allowed him to use the title 'Freiherr von'. On 25 October, Oberleutnant Oskar Freiherr von Boenigk was awarded Germany's highest accolade, the *Pour le Mérite*. By the end of the war he had raised his score to 26, but his days of action were not over and he served in the post-war revolution with some distinction.

During the Second World War, Boenigk served in the Luftwaffe as commander of various airfields, then as area commander, attaining the rank of Generalmajor. He was captured by the Russians in May 1945 and died in a prison camp the following year.

## Leutnant der Reserve Erwin BÖHME
(1879–1917)

Erwin Böhme was born in Holzminden, on the Weser, on 29 July 1879. After finishing school, he went to Dortmund and studied engineering at the technical college. On qualifying, Böhme worked in Elberfeld, Germany and Zürich, Switzerland, before going to East Africa. It was while in East Africa, whilst supervising the construction of a cable-car between Usambara and the New Hornow heights, that Böhme learned to fly, a skill he was to put to use some years later. Böhme had just returned to Germany when the war broke out and he immediately volunteered to join a *Jäger* Regiment. In the spring of 1915 he volunteered for flying duties with the newly formed German Army Air Service and because of his experience as a pilot, was accepted and retained as an instructor. This was not quite what Böhme had in mind, but a staunch defender of the Fatherland, he realised that this role was just as important.

In June 1916 Böhme applied for a posting to a front line unit and because there was a sudden desperate need for experienced pilots on the front, he was posted at the end of July to *Kasta* 10, a unit within *Kagohl* 2, commanded by Hauptmann Wilhelm Boelcke, brother of Oswald Boelcke. Böhme opened his tally on 2 August by shooting down a Nieuport XII whilst on patrol over Radzyse. Later that month he was introduced to Oswald Boelcke who was forming a new fighter unit, *Jasta* 2. The two of them hit it off right away and quickly became friends. Boelcke asked for Böhme to be assigned to his *Jasta* and by the beginning of September the *Jasta* was ready for action. On 17 September Böhme scored his second victory, a Sopwith 1½-Strutter from 70 Squadron, RFC, whilst on patrol over Hervilly, and was awarded the Iron Cross 2nd Class.

On 28 October tragedy struck for Böhme. With his tally now standing at five, he was on patrol with his friend Oswald Boelcke and Manfred von Richthofen, when they joined in a skirmish with DH2s from 24 Squadron, RFC. Böhme and Boelcke dived in tandem on one

*Portrait of Leutnant Erwin Böhme. Among the medal ribbons Böhme is wearing on his left breast, is one for the Knight's Cross with Swords of the Hohenzollern House Order. He is also wearing the Iron Cross 1st Class just above his pilot's badge.*

*Manfred von Richthofen visiting with other pilots. L–R: Leutnant Brauneck; Manfred von Richthofen; Albrecht von Richthofen (Manfred's father); Leutnant Erwin Böhme and Leutnant Kreft.*

of the British fighters, then suddenly another British fighter, hotly pursued by Richthofen, cut across their path. Böhme banked sharply, as did Boelcke, but they touched and Boelcke's upper wing was badly damaged. The speed at which they were travelling at the time caused the wind to rip the fabric off Boelcke's wing. Böhme managed to keep control of his aircraft, but Boelcke's aircraft plunged to the ground, killing him instantly. Böhme was devastated and blamed himself, but a board of enquiry cleared him of all blame. Böhme then dedicated himself to continuing the fight for the fatherland. By the end of the year he had raised his tally to eight. On 7 January 1917, he opened the new year by shooting down a DH.2 from 32 Squadron, RFC, whilst on patrol over Beugny. Victories on 4 February, another DH.2 from 32 Squadron, RFC, and a BE2c from 15 Squadron, RFC, brought his score to 11. Then on 11 February he was wounded in a scrap with a Sopwith 1½-Strutter and although he managed to get away, he was hospitalised for a month. Whilst in hospital he was awarded the Iron Cross 1st Class, which was followed on 12 March by the award of the Knight's Cross with Swords of the Hohenzollern House Order.

On being released from hospital at the end of March, Böhme was given the post of instructor as part of his recuperation. Then on 2 July he was posted to *Jasta* 29 as commander, but only managed to claim one more victory before being posted back to *Jasta* 2 as its commander. He was wounded again on 10 August 1917, when his aircraft was shot up by a Sopwith Camel whilst he was in the process of attacking a two-seater bomber. The wound was to his hand and kept him behind his desk at *Jasta* 2 for a month. Two more kills in September and six in October brought his tally to 21. On 6 November he shot down a Sopwith Camel from 65 Squadron, RFC, followed by a Nieuport Scout from No.1 Belgian *Escadrille*. Then on 24 November he was awarded Germany's highest decoration, the *Pour le Mérite*. He was to enjoy fame for only a few days, for on 29 November, whilst on patrol over Zonnebeke, his flight was attacked by a patrol from 10 Squadron, RFC. During the action Böhme shot down a Sopwith Camel, but failed to see the AWFK.8 behind him. Seconds later he was dead and his plane crashed behind British lines. Two days later he was buried by the British with full military honours at Keerselaarhook; his remains were reinterred at Hinter den Linden after the war.

## Rittmeister Karl BOLLE
(1893–1955)

Karl Bolle was born in Berlin on 20 June 1893, the son of an academic. After finishing school in Berlin, Bolle went to Oxford University in 1912 to read economics. Just before the outbreak of the First World War he returned to Germany and joined the 7th von Seydlitz *Kürassier* Regiment with the rank of Leutnant; almost immediately he was in France fighting on the Western Front. At the beginning of 1915 the regiment was moved to the Eastern Front, and was fighting in Poland and Courland. At the end of 1915, after receiving the Iron Cross 2nd Class, Bolle decided that he had had enough of the cold and the mud and applied for transfer to the newly formed German Army Air Service. His application was accepted and in February 1916 he was posted to Valenciennes for flying training.

On completion of his training in July 1915, he was awarded his pilot's badge and posted to KG4 as a reconnaissance pilot. After spending several months carrying out scouting and reconnaissance missions, Bolle was posted to *Kampfstaffel* 23 at the end of 1915 and was awarded the Wurttemburg Friedrich Order and the Knight 2nd Class with Swords. It was at *Kampfstaffel* 23 that he met his new observer, Lothar von Richthofen. Throughout 1916 they carried out many dangerous reconnaissance flights and on one of them, in October 1916, Bolle was badly wounded. On his return two months

*Unser erfolgreicher Kampfflieger Leutnant Karl Bolle*

*Portrait of Rittmeister Karl Bolle as a Leutnant. He is wearing the medal ribbons of the Württemberg Friedrich Order and the Knight 2nd Class with Swords. On his left breast can be seen the Iron Cross 1st Class just above his pilot's badge.*

later, he found that the application he had made some months earlier to transfer to single-seater fighters had been accepted, and he was posted to *Jastaschule* at the beginning of 1917.

After graduating in July 1917, he was posted to *Jasta* 28. On 8 August he opened his tally by shooting down a DH.4 from 57 Squadron RFC, whilst on patrol over Kachtem. His second kill, a Martinsyde G100 bomber from 27 Squadron RFC, was shot down over Seclin on 21 August. It was not until 18 December that he scored his next victory, a Sopwith Camel from 65 Squadron RFC. On 29 January 1918, Bolle scored his fourth victory when he shot down another Sopwith Camel from 65 Squadron. The following day he raised his tally to five by shooting down a DH.4 from 5 Squadron, RNAS. Despite his relative inexperience, Bolle was given command of *Jasta* 2 on 20 February 1918 and promoted to Oberleutnant. He immediately set about making it one of the best, but it was to be two months before Bolle himself got back into the air and started scoring again. On 3 April he shot down a DH.9 bomber whilst on patrol over Frezenberg, and on 25 April a Sopwith Camel, raising his tally to seven.

The next three months of the war in the air were frantic ones. The Allies started making their big push and the skies were cluttered with aircraft. By the end of July, Bolle had shot down a further 21 Allied aircraft, bringing his score to 28, but at an even greater cost to his own squadrons. He was promoted to Rittmeister at the beginning of August and awarded the Order of Max Joseph, the Mecklenburg Military Cross of Merit with Swords and the Knight's Cross with Swords of the Hohenzollern House Order. Then on 28 August 1918, he received the ultimate accolade, the *Pour le Mérite*. Bolle continued to fight on and by the end of the war had raised his score to 36.

On leaving the Army, Bolle became an instructor, then in the early 1920s was appointed Director of the German Transportation Flying School, in charge of all pilot training. When the Second World War started, Bolle became special adviser to the Luftwaffe, a post he held throughout the war. Karl Bolle died in Berlin on 9 October 1955.

## Leutnant der Reserve Heinrich BONGARTZ
(1892–1946)

The son of a schoolteacher, Heinrich Bongartz was born in Gelsenkirchen, Westphalia, on 31 January 1892. Throughout his childhood it was obvious that he would follow the family tradition and become a schoolteacher. But like many other boys of his generation, his life was to be affected by the actions of a young Bosnian man by the name of Gavrilo Princip, who, on the morning of 28 June 1914, in Sarajevo, Bosnia-Herzegovina, was to commit an act that would affect the lives of millions of other people – the assassination of the Archduke Ferdinand and his wife the Duchess Sophie.

*Portrait of Leutnant Heinrich Bongartz wearing his* Pour le Mérite *and the medal ribbons of the Iron Cross and the Knight's Cross with Swords of the Hohenzollern House Order.*

Unser erfolgreicher Kampfflieger
Leutnant Bongartz

After leaving school, Bongartz went to college and trained as a teacher. Then in August 1914, at the outbreak of war, he volunteered for the army and joined Infantry Regiment Nr.16, then later the Reserve Infantry Regiment Nr.13 with the rank of Sturmoffizier. The regiment was stationed on the Western Front near Verdun and, throughout 1915, Bongartz saw some of the heaviest fighting of the war. In March 1916 his bravery and leadership qualities earned him a commission as Leutnant and the award of the Iron Cross 2nd Class. But the fighting in the mud and cold had taken its toll on him, so he applied for transfer to the German Army Air Service. He was accepted and posted for training as a pilot to FA 5 in the autumn of 1916. On completion of his training in the October, he was posted to *Kaghol* 5 as a reconnaissance and scouting pilot. At the beginning of January 1917, he was posted to *Kasta* 27 (which later became *Schusta* 8) where he stayed until the beginning of April 1917 when he was posted to *Jasta* 36.

*Sopwith Triplane No. 5350.*

Within days of arriving at *Jasta* 36, Bongartz had opened his tally when he shot down a Spad V.II from Spa 31, whilst on patrol over Viry. By the end of the month he had increased his score to four. He continued to score steadily until 13 July when, with his tally standing at 11, he was wounded in a battle with Allied fighters. The wound put him out of commission for two months, but on 26 September he celebrated his return by shooting down a Sopwith Triplane over Houthulst Forest. At the end of September Bongartz became the Commanding Officer of *Jasta* 36. In the following two months he scored another 14 victories, bringing his total to 25 and the award of the Knight's Cross with Swords of the Hohenzollern House Order. Bongartz finished the year by shooting down another two Allied fighters and raising his tally to 27. On 23 December 1917, he was awarded Germany's highest honour, the *Pour le Mérite*.

The new year started quietly for Bongartz, with only one victory on 29 January, a Sopwith Camel whilst on patrol over Poelkapelle. Two more in February and three in March took his score to 33, then on 29 March he was wounded in action. The following month, on 25 April, he was slightly injured again, but on 29 April he was very seriously wounded. Whilst on patrol over Kemmel Hill, he clashed with fighters from 74 Squadron, RFC, and during the mêlée, he was hit in the head. The bullet passed right through his left temple, his eye and his nose. His aircraft crashed near Kemmel Hill and he was taken unconscious to hospital. The wounds were so serious that he lost his left eye, which finished his wartime career. He later took over as Director of the Aeroplane Inspectorate at Aldershorf, where he stayed until the end of the war and helped to deactivate the German Army Flying Corps.

During the post-war revolution Bongartz fought against the Spartacists, a group of German left-wingers who formed the nucleus of the German Communist Party. But again he was seriously wounded, this time in the leg. His military career was finally finished and he was invalided out, but Bongartz could not stay away from aviation and became the Director of German Air Trade (*Luftreederei*), a department that was concerned with using airships for trade and transport. In January 1921 he was involved in a crash and again was severely injured, but recovered later in the year. Heinrich Bongartz died of a heart attack on 23 January 1946.

## Hauptmann Ernst BRANDENBURG
(1883–1952)

Destined to become one of the oldest pilots in the First World War, Ernst Brandenburg was born on 4 June 1883 in Westphalia. On leaving school, Ernst Brandenburg joined the Army as a cadet and, after graduating, joined the 6th West Prussian Infantry Regiment Nr.149 based in Schneidemühl. In 1911 he was assigned to the Research Institute for the Aviation System to study the merits of military aviation. He progressed steadily in the Army and, at the outbreak of war in 1914, was an Oberleutnant and the Regimental Adjutant. The regiment was soon in action on the Western Front and the sight of reconnaissance aircraft spotting for the infantry quickly rekindled Brandenburg's interest in aviation. After just over a year on the front, in which he was awarded the Iron Cross 2nd Class after being seriously wounded, Brandenburg was declared unfit for the trenches. He then applied for transfer to the German Army Air Service on 1 November 1915 and was accepted.

After graduating as an observer in the spring of 1916, Ernst Brandenburg was assigned to a reconnaissance unit attached to the infantry. He carried out numerous missions for which he was awarded the Iron Cross 1st Class and the Knight's Cross of the Hohenzollern House Order. Then on 10 January 1917, he was asked by General Hoeppner to form a bomber squadron for the express purpose of carrying out raids against the British, the main target

*Portrait shot of Hauptmann Ernst Brandenburg wearing his Pour le Mérite and the medal ribbon of the Knight's Cross with Swords of the Hohenzollern House Order. On his lower left breast can be seen his Iron Cross 1st Class and his observer's badge.*

being London. These raids were to be the first of their kind and posed numerous problems, the main ones being the unreliability of the aircraft and the weather. Brandenburg formed up the squadron, *Kagohl* 3, also known as the *England Geschwader*, and started intense training with the air and ground crews. He discovered that the fuel carried by the Gotha bombers was not sufficient to complete the round trip, so auxiliary tanks were fitted. The Gotha's attack altitude of 14,000 feet afforded it a large degree of protection and once it had unloaded its bombs, it could climb even higher. To protect the three-man crews from the elements, each member of the crew was given extra thick clothing and the bombers were equipped with two small cylinders of compressed oxygen. A rubber pipe was attached and the crew members sucked on it just like they would on an oriental pipe. Many pilots said that they would just have preferred a swig of cognac.

Although *Kagohl* 3 was attached to the German Fourth Army, it operated independently and received its orders from OHL (*Oberste Heeresleitung*). At the beginning of June 1917, Brandenburg decided that they were ready and planned the first raid. The unpredictable British weather intervened, not once but twice, then on 13 June, although the weather was inclement, Brandenburg decided to delay no longer. At 10.00 a.m., 18 Gotha bombers took off from Ghent and headed across the English Channel. As they crossed the coast the alarm bells started ringing in England and at 1.00 p.m. the aircraft appeared over London. They immediately encountered anti-aircraft fire from the defences around London, but it was ineffective. The guns had been poorly positioned and the crews even more poorly trained. The bombers started unloading their deadly cargoes on predetermined targets, destroying docks, railway stations and warehouses. Of the 30 British fighters scrambled to intercept them, not one was effective. A number of the Gothas were hit but two hours after bombing London the entire squadron landed in Ghent.

The following day, 14 June, Brandenburg was summoned to Supreme Headquarters and in front of the Kaiser and all the warlords, described the raid in detail. He was promoted to Hauptmann and the Kaiser personally awarded Brandenburg Germany's highest award, the *Pour le Mérite* and invited him to stay the weekend. Early on the following Tuesday, Brandenburg's Albatros aircraft, with his pilot Oberleutnant Freiherr von Trotha at the controls, took off. As the aircraft lifted from the runway the engine spluttered and the Albatros plunged into the ground. Brandenburg was pulled from the wreckage with severe injuries, including a shattered leg which was later amputated.

*Gotha bomber being fuelled up for a bombing mission on London.*

*German Gothas in front of airship hangar at Gontrode.*

After recuperating he returned to the squadron and organised other raids, but his days were numbered and he was taken off active service duty. At the end of the war his squadron was disbanded and Brandenburg returned to Germany. In 1924 he became the Director of Civil Aviation, a department within the transport ministry, under whose umbrella the Luftwaffe was born. Former senior army officers were enrolled in commercial pilot schools and over 27 million marks were channelled to the *Reichswehr* through the ministry for military aviation. With the rise of the Nazis, Brandenburg was pushed aside in favour of Ernst Udet and faded into obscurity. He died in 1952 in Berlin.

### Leutnant Franz BÜCHNER
(1898–1920)

Franz Büchner was born on 2 January 1898 in Leipzig, the son of a wealthy businessman. At the onset of war in 1914, Büchner was only 16 but he joined up immediately with the 106th Saxon Infantry Regiment. The regiment was soon in action in Ypres and Büchner was already showing his leadership qualities, even at that early age. In November 1914 he contracted typhoid fever and it was not until February 1915 that he was able to rejoin his regiment. The regiment moved to the Russian Front in March and in August Büchner was commissioned. Moving back to France in the September with his regiment, he was awarded the Iron Cross 2nd Class after being involved in a number of actions. On 3 April 1916 he was wounded during a battle on the Western Front and it was while in hospital recuperating that he decided to ask for a transfer to the German Army Air Service. Büchner was accepted and posted to FFA 270 for training as a pilot. On graduating in July 1916, he was posted to *Jasta* 9 flying single-seater aircraft, but had very little success. In fact he had only one kill in the period from July 1916 to August 1917, and that was a Nieuport fighter on 17 August whilst on patrol over Chappy.

In the October, Büchner was posted to *Jasta* 13 and although he was still experiencing difficulties in shooting down Allied aircraft, his leadership qualities were showing through. Then on 10 and 11 June he increased his score by bringing down two Spads whilst on patrol over Vauxaillion. Büchner was appointed Staffelführer on 15 June, despite only having scored four victories, such was the high regard in which he was held. His scoring rate started to improve rapidly in July and by the end of the month his total had risen to 12. Büchner was awarded the Iron Cross 1st Class in August, followed by the Knight's Cross with Swords of the Hohenzollern House Order and the Saxon Merit Order 2nd Class with Swords. He celebrated these awards by shooting down another eight Allied aircraft, bringing his tally to 20 by the end of August.

On 12 September 1918 Büchner shot down a DH.4 from the 8th Aero Squadron USAS whilst on patrol over Hattonville. This was one of the first contacts the Germans had with the Americans and it was not going to be the last. Also on that day he shot down another DH.4 and a Breguet XIV bomber. By the end of September, Büchner had become the scourge of the US Aero Squadrons and had shot down 18 of their aircraft, bringing his personal tally to 37. For this achievement he was awarded the Military St Heinrich's Order (Saxony's highest award) and the Saxon Albert Order 2nd Class with Swords.

October started well for Büchner with the shooting down of a Salmson 2A2 bomber, but on 10 October a collision with one of his fellow pilots nearly ended his life. Both aircraft were attacking an Allied bomber when they collided in mid-air. The pilots took to their parachutes and fortunately for them both the parachutes opened (a rarity in those early days) taking them safely to the ground. Büchner managed to add another two kills to his score before the war ended. On 25 October at the age of 20 he was awarded Germany's highest award, the *Pour le Mérite*, the ultimate accolade to a top fighter pilot whose tally of victories at the end of the war numbered 40.

*Head and shoulders portrait shot of Leutnant Franz Büchner wearing his* Pour le Mérite.

The war may have ended in Europe for the Allies, but it still continued within Germany as the post-war revolutionaries attempted to take over. Büchner continued to fight on with the Reichswehr, but on 18 March 1920 he was shot down and killed whilst on a reconnaissance flight near his home town of Leipzig. Like Rudolf Berthold, he was killed by his own countrymen, something the British, French and Americans had failed to do in four years of intensive fighting.

### Leutnant der Reserve Julius BUCKLER
(1894–1960)

Julius Buckler was born in Mainz on 28 March 1894. He was a bright schoolboy who had aspirations to be an architect. At 15 he went to work for a short time with Anthony Fokker, the Dutch aircraft builder and designer, in his design office, but circumstances at home were instrumental in him joining the Army. In 1913 Buckler joined the Infantry Line Regiment Nr. 117 as the war clouds gathered. Within days of the outbreak of the First World War, Buckler and his regiment were in action on the Western Front. Within a few weeks, for meritorious service, Buckler received the Iron Cross 2nd Class. Then in August he was badly wounded and after being released from hospital in October 1914, was deemed to be unfit for army service. But Buckler, despite having been involved in some of the heaviest fighting and having suffered some terrible injuries, wanted to be part of the war.

In November 1914 he volunteered for flying duties and was accepted for training as an observer. He joined FEA 6 at Leipzig-Lindenthal two weeks later and after only four weeks' instruction, passed his flight exams. Such was the natural aptitude and ability of Buckler that he remained at FEA 6 as an instructor. After spending just over six months at FEA 6, he was posted to FA(A) 209 as an observer. Buckler spent nearly a year with FA(A) 209, in which he was awarded the Iron Cross 1st Class, but then in the spring of 1916 he requested pilot training. He was accepted and on completion of his training in the November, Buckler was posted to *Jasta* 17 with the rank of Vizefeldwebel and almost immediately was in action over Verdun. On 17 December he opened his tally by shooting down a twin-engined Caudron whilst on patrol over Bras.

Two more Caudrons on 14 and 15 February brought his score to three and by the end of April he had raised it to six. Buckler continued to score steadily until 17 July 1917, when, whilst on patrol over Keyem with his *Jasta*, they ran into a patrol of Sopwith Camels and

*Portrait of Julius Buckler wearing his* Pour le Mérite, Iron Cross 1st Class and Golden Military Merit badge.

Pups. After shooting down one Sopwith Pup, Buckler was badly wounded in a fight with another, but he managed to break away and return to his field. Then on 12 August, with his score standing at 13, he was once more shot and wounded in a tussle with a Sopwith Camel, but again managed to break away and return to his field. On 12 November, after his 25th victory, he was promoted to Leutnant and awarded the Golden Military Service Cross. He celebrated this by shooting down an RE.8 from 21 Squadron, RFC, on 15 November 1917, followed by two balloons and an RE.8 on 18 November. Buckler crashed on 30 November after being attacked by Allied fighters, surviving an horrendous plummet to the ground from 800 metres. Considering the fall his injuries were extremely light – two broken arms and numerous bruises. His score at this time stood at 30, and on 4 December, whilst he was in hospital, he was awarded Germany's highest award – the *Pour le Mérite*. This award made him one of only five airmen to be awarded the *Pour le Mérite* <u>and</u> the Gold Military Service Cross.

Buckler returned to *Jasta* 17 at the beginning of April 1918 and was soon back in action. On 16 April he shot down a Breguet XIV whilst on patrol over Vaux, and on 21 April another Breguet XIV over Mareuil. Buckler was wounded once more on 6 May, this time in the ankle. It was a wound that was to put him in hospital for nearly eight weeks and was to win him the award of a Golden Wound Badge – his fifth wound. He returned to *Jasta* 17 at the beginning of July and fortunately settled down to a period of inactivity. Then on 22 September 1918 he was made Staffelführer, a post he held until the end of the war. His tally at the end of hostilities stood at 36.

During the Second World War, Julius Buckler served with training squadrons of the Luftwaffe. He died in Berlin on 23 May 1960, one of the few pilots to make it through two world wars.

## Hauptmann Hans-Joachim BUDDECKE
(1890–1918)

The son of an Army General Staff Officer, Hans-Joachim Buddecke was born in Berlin on 22 August 1890. After leaving school in 1904, at the age of 14, he joined the Army as a cadet and was commissioned as a Leutnant in 1910 at the age of 20. After three years he resigned his commission and went to work for his uncle in America, as an engineer in his car plant. One year later Buddecke had earned enough to buy a second-hand French Nieuport aeroplane and set about learning to fly. Buddecke soon became very competent and could see that there was going to be a great future in aviation. With the help of his uncle he decided to set up his own factory and build aircraft to his own design. But the First World War erupted in Europe and he made his way back to Germany aboard a Greek freighter.

At the beginning of June 1915, Buddecke joined the German

Pilots of Jasta 18 with Hauptmann Hans-Joachim Buddecke (3rd from right) and Hauptmann Rudolf Berthold (5th from right).

Army Air Service and was given the rank of Leutnant because of his previous army experience. After a brief period at *Jastaschule*, he was posted to FA 23 as a scout and reconnaissance pilot flying Fokkers. Here he became close friends with Rudolf Berthold, and it was when flying with him on patrol that he claimed his first victory. The patrol

Hauptmann Hans-Joachim Buddecke seen here wearing his Balkan hat whilst serving in Turkey.

was flying over St Quentin when they sighted a patrol of British aircraft from 8 Squadron, RFC. As the two patrols closed on each other, Berthold came under attack from a BE2c. Quickly Buddecke closed on the British aircraft and shot it down – it was to be the first of many. Buddecke scored a second BE2c on 23 October and a third one on 11 November, bringing his tally to three by the end of the year and the award of the Iron Cross 2nd Class.

At the end of December Buddecke was posted to Gallipoli with Ottoman FA 6 flying Halberstadt D.IIs, D.Vs, and Fokker E.IIIs as a scout and reconnaissance pilot, and was promoted to Oberleutnant. FA 6 was based at Smyrna and was heavily involved in the evacuation from Gallipoli. On 6 January Buddecke scored his fourth victory, a Maurice Farman from 2 Squadron, RNAS, over Cape Narors. By the end of the month he had raised his total to seven and had been awarded the Silver

Liaket Medal and the Iron Cross 1st Class. At the end of April 1916, he was awarded the coveted *Pour le Mérite*, the Golden Liaket Medal, the Saxon Military St Heinrich's Order 4th Class and the Knight's Cross with Swords of the Hohenzollern House Order. The Turks had nicknamed him 'The Shooting Hawk' and 'The Hunting Hawk'.

Buddecke was posted back to France at the beginning of August, where he was appointed Staffeführer of *Jasta* 4 on 28 August 1916 and promoted to Hauptmann. He increased his tally during September to 10, but was then posted back to Turkey in the middle of December to join Ottoman FA 5. The rest of 1916 was extremely quiet for Buddecke and his flying consisted mainly of scouting and reconnaissance missions. He became more active in March 1917 when, on the 30th, whilst on patrol over Smyrna, he came across a patrol of British reconnaissance fighter-bombers. After a short skirmish, Buddecke shot down a Farman F27 and a Nieuport XII from 2 Squadron, RNAS, raising his score to 12. Things quietened down again and for the rest of the year he flew reconnaissance and scouting missions.

At the beginning of 1918 he received a message from his friend Rudolph Berthold, who was now commander of *Jasta* 18, asking him to join him as his deputy. Buddecke, tired of the inactivity in Turkey, immediately accepted the offer from his friend and arranged for a posting to *Jasta* 18. He returned to France at the beginning of February, going first to *Jasta* 30 for a couple of days, then on to *Jasta* 18. On 19 February 1918, whilst on patrol over Neuve Chapelle, he shot down a Sopwith Camel from 80 Squadron, RFC. But the long periods of inactivity in Turkey were showing and on 10 March 1918, whilst on patrol with his friend Berthold, his luck ran out. The patrol was over Harmes when it ran into a patrol of Sopwith Camels from 3 Squadron, RNAS. Buddecke was flying as wingman to Berthold when Berthold was attacked. Buddecke went to his aid, but was caught by another Sopwith Camel. His lack of combat experience during the long periods of inactivity caught up with him and he was shot down. He was buried in Berlin with full military honours on 22 March 1918.

## Leutnant Walter von BÜLOW-BOTHKAMP
(1894–1918)

Walter von Bülow-Bothkamp was born on 24 April 1894 at Borby, near Eckernförde, Holstein. He was the son of a very wealthy landowner whose family had a strong military background. Von

Bülow was a very bright pupil and when he finished school he broke the family tradition and went to study law at Heidelberg University. At the onset of war, however, he joined the famous Saxon Hussar Regiment Nr.17, 'The Death's Head' Hussars, whose commander had once been the legendary Feldmarschall August von Mackensen. The Hussars were very soon in action, then later, early in 1915, they saw heavy fighting in the Alsace Region. Walter von Bülow stood out from the rest of the men and after a series of skirmishes in which he distinguished himself, he was given a field commission as Leutnant and was awarded the Iron Cross 2nd Class.

But even at this early stage of the war von Bülow could see that the future of the Hussars was in doubt. The days of the cavalry wearing elaborate uniforms and charging with lance and sword were gone, and mechanisation was the key to victory. In the spring of 1915 von Bülow applied for transfer to the newly formed German Army Air Service and was accepted. He was posted to Valenciennes for

pilot training in the June, and on graduating was assigned to FA 22 flying reconnaissance missions in twin-engined AEG GII biplanes. On 10 October 1915 von Bülow opened his tally when he shot down a Voisin whilst flying on a reconnaissance mission over Metz. The next day he scored another victory, a Maurice Farman whilst patrolling the Champagne region, and for the two victories was awarded the Iron Cross 1st Class.

In the January of 1916 Leutnant Walter von Bülow was posted to FA 300 in Palestine. It was a welcome relief as far as the weather was concerned, but there was comparatively very little action. It was not until 8 August that von Bülow scored his next victory, an EA over El Arish, Suez, and then on 17 September two Sopwith Babies, the first one being from the seaplane carrier *Ben-my-Chree*, again over El Arish. Von Bülow was posted back to the Western Front to join *Jasta* 18 in December 1916, after numerous requests.

Von Bülow took his tally to six on 23 January 1917 when he shot down a Sopwith 1½-Strutter from 45 Squadron, RFC, and an FE8 from 41 Squadron, whilst patrolling over Gheluvelt in his Albatros

*Portrait of Leutnant Walter von Bülow-Bothkamp relaxing in his chair with his pet dog, wearing his Pour le Mérite and Iron Cross 1st Class. It is interesting to note that he is wearing the Skull and Crossbones of his old regiment, the Saxon Hussar Regiment Nr.17 (The Death's Head Hussars), in his cap.*

D.V. By the end of April he had increased his score to 12 and had been awarded the Knight's Cross with Swords of the Hohenzollern House Order and the Saxon Military St Heinrich's Order. This was followed on 10 May by him being appointed commander of *Jasta* 36. Von Bülow continued to score regularly and by the beginning of October 1917 he had raised his tally to 21. On 8 October he was awarded Germany's highest honour, the *Pour le Mérite*. Von Bülow's score kept mounting and when on 13 December he was made commander of *Jasta* 2 (Boelcke), it had reached 28.

But his appointment as commander of the prestigious 'Boelcke' *Jasta* was not to last long. Whilst on patrol in his Albatros D.V over Ypres, east of Passendale, his patrol was jumped by British fighters from 23 and 70 Squadrons RFC. After a brief fight, Leutnant Walter von Bülow's aircraft was seen to spin out of control into the front-line trenches. His body was recovered and buried with full military honours. He was aged 24.


## Kapitänleutnant Horst Freiherr Treusch von BUTTLAR-BRANDENFELS
(1888–1943)

Horst Treusch von Buttlar-Brandenfels was born on 14 June 1888 in Hannau, Darmstadt. After finishing high school in Darmstadt, he followed the family tradition and joined the Imperial German Navy in 1903 as a sea cadet. On completion of his initial training, Buttlar-Brandenfels was commissioned in the rank of Leutnant zur See and sent on a radio-telephony course. Upon graduating he was posted as RT Officer to the staff of the Commander of the Reconnaissance Ships. The Zeppelins at that time were beginning to show their worth and flight trials were begun in 1910, with the intention of using the Zeppelin as an aerial scouting ship for the Navy.

The first air-to-ship radio test flight was with the L2 airship, but because of the extra equipment aboard, some of the crew were scratched from the flight, including Buttlar-Brandenfels. During the trials the airship crashed, killing all on board. Later trials were relatively successful and during the Battle of Jutland the Zeppelins were used extensively to radio back the positions of the British Fleet.

Buttlar-Brandenfels decided to become an airship pilot and soon after applying for training was accepted. Not long after he had graduated from training school, the war clouds that had been threatening

Europe broke, and soon all the major European powers were at war. At the age of 26, Buttlar-Brandenfels was given command of his first airship, the L6. His first contact with the enemy was on Christmas Day 1914, when, whilst on patrol off Helgoland, he sighted three minelayers accompanied by two cruisers and eight destroyers. Buttlar-Brandenfels attempted to send a radio message, but his equipment was out of order. Not content to sit back and watch the minelayers continue their deadly work, he decided to attack and from a height of over 4,000 feet dropped three 110lb bombs. The bombs did no damage and only succeeded in drawing some very accurate fire from the accompanying cruisers. Buttlar-Brandenfels withdrew his airship into the clouds, then using them as cover, came in low, strafing the ships with machine-gun fire from the two gondolas and the upper gun platform. The ships returned fire and punctured the airship repeatedly, forcing Buttlar-Brandenfels to abandon his attack and turn for home. The airship began to lose height, obliging him to dump all his gasoline tanks, but he still managed to drop a message to the battleship *Seydlitz* as they passed overhead. He received the Iron Cross 2nd Class for this mission and promotion to Kommander.

*Portrait shot of Kapitänleutnant Horst Freiherr von Buttlar-Brandenfels in naval uniform wearing his* Pour le Mérite.

On 19 January 1915 Buttlar-Brandenfels, with his airship L6, awaited orders to carry out the first attack on Britain. Just after crossing the coast he had to return because of engine trouble. It wasn't until 17 August that he was to carry out his first successful raid, this time in the airship L11. Before the end of the war, Buttlar-Brandenfels was to fly more than 19 missions to England, be awarded the Iron Cross 1st Class and be promoted to Kapitänleutnant. After the fifteenth mission he was awarded Germany's highest award, the *Pour le Mérite*, whilst his crew each received the Iron Cross 1st Class.

At the end of the war Buttlar-Brandenfels was one of those responsible for destroying the entire airship fleet at Nordholz in defiance of the Versailles Treaty. During the Second World War he served with the Luftwaffe and was killed in action.

## Kapitänleutnant zur See Friedrich CHRISTIANSEN
(1879–1972)

The son of a sea captain, Friedrich Christiansen was born at Wyk on Föhr on 12 December 1879. The naval tradition in the family made it obvious where Friedrich Christiansen's future lay. On leaving school in 1895, he joined the merchant marines where he served for seven years before volunteering for military service in 1901 serving on MTBs.

After one year Christiansen returned to the merchant marine where he served for several more years, becoming second officer of the five-masted sailing ship *Preussen*, the largest sailing ship in the world. Then in 1913 he decided to deviate from his career and learned to fly. After graduating and gaining his licence, No.707, he became an instructor at a civilian flying school. At the outbreak of the First World War, in August 1914, Christiansen was called up and was posted to Zeebrugge as a naval aviator. For the first year he was flying

*Portrait of Christiansen wearing his Pour le Mérite.*

Brandenburg W12 seaplanes on missions over the North Sea and Britain. He even carried out a bombing mission on Dover and Ramsgate for which he was awarded the Iron Cross 2nd Class. For the next year he went on numerous reconnaissance and bombing missions, making the *C-Staffel* at Zeebrugge one of the most successful units in the German Naval Air Service. On 27 April 1916, as Leutnant der Matrosen Artillerie (Lieutenant of Naval Artillery), Friedrich Christiansen was awarded the Iron Cross 1st Class and the Knight's Cross with Swords of the Hohenzollern House Order.

Christiansen claimed his first victory on 15 May 1917, when he shot down a Sopwith Pup whilst on patrol off Dover. On 1 September 1917 he took command of the Naval Air Station at Zeebrugge and was promoted to Oberleutnant. He celebrated this appointment by shooting down a Porte FB2 Baby, off Felixstowe. Fortunately for the crew of this flying boat, they were able to land on the water and taxi back into Felixstowe harbour. Christiansen continued to carry out recon-

Shot of the C27 coastal airship going down in flames after being shot down by Christiansen flying a Brandenburg floatplane.

Friedrich Christiansen wearing the uniform of the NSFK (National Socialist Flying Korps). His Pour le Mérite can be clearly seen around his neck.

naissance, rescue and bombing missions and by December 1917 had completed 440 missions, including the shooting down of Airship C27. At the end of December he was awarded Germany's highest award, the *Pour le Mérite*.

Christiansen increased his tally on 15 February 1918 when he shot down a Curtiss H12B flying boat from Felixstowe. This was followed by two more Curtiss H12Bs on 24 and 25 April. In June and July he claimed three more flying boats, all Felixstowe F2As. Then on 6 July, while Christiansen was on patrol in the Thames Estuary, he surprised the British submarine C-25 cruising on the surface. He attacked the submarine, killing the captain and five crewmen. He thought he had sunk the submarine, but in fact she managed to limp back, with great difficulty, to harbour.

By the end of the war, Christiansen had raised his personal tally to 13, but this is speculative because there were possibly shared victories. Christiansen returned to the merchant marine for a while before taking a post as a pilot for the Dornier Company. It was whilst with Dorniers, that he flew the largest

*This remarkable photo, taken from another aircraft, shows Christiansen attacking the British submarine C-25.*

seaplane in the world at that time, the Dornier Do.X, on its maiden Atlantic flight to New York in 1930.

In 1933 Christiansen joined the German Aviation Ministry as it struggled to rebuild its air force. He was appointed Korpsführer of the National Socialist Flying Korps (NSFK) at its conception in 1937. Two years later when war was again declared and the German Army occupied Holland, Christiansen was appointed officer commanding occupied Holland, a post he held until the end of the war when he was imprisoned by the Allies. On his release from prison he retired to West Germany and died at Innien in December 1972 at the age of 93, an incredible age for someone who had lived and fought through two world wars.

### Leutnant Carl DEGELOW
(1891–1970)

Carl Degelow was born on 5 January 1891 in Münsterdorf, Germany. The urge to travel which had gripped him throughout his childhood resulted in him going to America when he was 21, where he had various jobs throughout the United States from Chicago to El Paso, Texas. Carl Degelow returned to Germany after hearing that there was possibly going to be a war in Europe and arrived back just prior to the start of the First World War.

*Leutnant Carl Degelow standing beside his Fokker D.VII bearing his personal 'Stag' insignia on the fuselage.*

*Leutnant Carl Degelow in the cockpit of a captured Bristol F2b fighter.*

At the onset of war, he joined the *Nassauische Infantrie-Regiment* Nr.88 and after training was sent to the Western Front. His regiment was in action almost immediately and Degelow showed his leadership qualities within weeks of being there. Within three months he had been promoted from Gefreiter to Unteroffizier and had been awarded the Iron Cross 2nd Class. At the beginning of 1915, the regiment was posted to the Russian Front. Once again Degelow showed his leadership qualities by leading a succession of fighting patrols against the Russians, for which he was promoted to Vizefeldwebel and awarded the Iron Cross 1st Class. It was on one of these patrols against the Russians that Degelow was badly wounded in the arm. On 31 July, whilst in hospital, he was awarded a commission to Leutnant, but his inclinations were to get away from the mud and cold of the Russian Front, so he decided to apply for a transfer to the German Army Air Service.

On release from hospital Leutnant Carl Degelow returned to the Russian Front. In April 1916 his transfer came through and he was posted to flying school back in Germany. After graduating at the beginning of 1917, he was posted to Flieger Abteilung (A) 216 on the Somme as a reconnaissance pilot. Together with his observer, Leutnant Kurten, he flew artillery support and reconnaissance missions in their Albatros C.V. Whilst on an artillery support flight over SW Braye, on 22 May 1917, they were attacked by a Caudron G.IV. During the ensuing dogfight they managed to get the better of it and shoot it down, but unfortunately it was unconfirmed. Three days later whilst on a reconnaissance mission over Bailly-Braye, they were attacked by another Caudron G.IV, which they also shot down, but this time it was confirmed and he had opened his tally.

Degelow applied for transfer to single-seater fighters and was posted to *Jasta* 36 for training, but within days he had been returned to his unit after accidentally shooting an airman whilst carrying out gunnery practice on the ground. On 17 August 1917 he was posted to *Jasta* 7 where he notched up another two victories, but again they were unconfirmed. But a victory on 25 January 1918, a F2b of 20 Squadron, another on 21 April, a Sopwith Camel from 54 Squadron and on 16 May an RE.8, raised his tally to four. Degelow was posted to *Jasta* 40 on 16 May 1918, taking command on 11 July. As if to celebrate his appointment as commander Degelow shot down six more aircraft in July, bringing his score to 13.

He was awarded the Knight's Cross with Swords of the Hohenzollern House Order on 9 August and promptly shot down another six Allied aircraft in the month of September. By the end of October he had shot down a further 10 Allied aircraft, raising his total to 29, and he made it 30 on 4 November 1918, when he shot down a DH.9 near the Dutch border. Then on 9 November he was awarded the *Pour le Mérite*, the last member of the German Army Air Service ever to receive the prestigious award.

After the war Degelow created the Hamburg *Zeitfreiwillingen Korps* and fought against the communists in the post-war revolution. At the beginning of the Second World War he joined the Luftwaffe, becoming a Major. After surviving a second world war, Degelow went into business and died in Hamburg on 9 November 1970.

## Leutnant der Reserve Albert DOSSENBACH
(1891–1917)

The son of a local hotel owner, Albert Dossenbach was born in St. Blasien in the southern part of the Black Forest on 5 June 1891. He intended to follow in his father's footsteps by attending medical school and was starting his hospital internship when war was declared. Dossenbach enlisted in the Army and because of his background and training was promoted to Unteroffizier within weeks. Four weeks after joining the Army, he was awarded the Iron Cross 2nd Class for carrying his commanding officer away from the Front Line to safety after he had been wounded. Within four months, after being involved in a number of missions, Dossenbach had been awarded the Iron Cross

*Leutnant Albert Dossenbach wearing his* Pour le Mérite, *standing beside his Albatros C.II. The scars on his face from his crash on 27 September 1916 can be clearly seen.*

1st Class, the Military Merit Cross and had been promoted to Feldwebel.

The new year started brightly for Dossenbach when he was commissioned to Leutnant on 27 January 1915, but by the end of the year his thoughts had turned to other things and he applied for transfer to the newly formed German Army Air Service. In the spring of 1916 he was posted to *Jastaschule* and graduated in June 1916. Posted to FA 22, he joined up with his new observer Hans Schilling and their Albatros C.II. They were in the thick of the action almost immediately and in the three months after graduating, Dossenbach and his observer were credited with shooting down eight Allied aircraft. The last of the eight victims, on 27 September, managed to inflict a considerable amount of damage to Dossenbach's aircraft before he crashed, the result being that Dossenbach had to crash-land. Both he and his observer were slightly burned in the ensuing fire, but were soon in action again. Dossenbach was awarded the Knight's Cross 2nd Class with Swords to the Order of the Zahringer Lion, and a month later, on the 21 October 1917, he was awarded the Knight's Cross of the Hohenzollern House Order. He promptly went out and shot down an FE2b of 25 Squadron whilst on patrol over Tourmignies; however, in the fight his observer was badly wounded, which took the edge off the celebrations.

On 11 November 1916 Leutnant Albert Dossenbach was awarded Germany's highest honour, the *Pour le Mérite*, the first two-seater pilot ever to receive this prestigious award. A further award was made on 9 December when he was given the Knight's Cross of the Karl Friedrich Military Merit Order, but this honour was overshadowed by the death of his friend and former observer Hans Schilling who was killed whilst on a bombing mission with another pilot. It was just after this that Dossenbach applied to go to *Jasta* 2 for single-seater training. After graduating he took command of *Jasta* 36 on 22 February 1917 and set the standard by scoring the unit's first victory, a French Caudron from *Escadrille* Spa.12 on 5 April. By the end of the month Dossenbach had raised his personal tally to 14.

A bombing attack on his airfield on 2 May left Dossenbach badly wounded from bomb splinters which put him in hospital for a month. On release from hospital he was given command of *Jasta* 10 and took up the post on 21 June. He opened his score with the *Jasta* on 27 June by shooting down an observation balloon over Ypres, raising his tally to 15. Then on 3 July 1917, whilst on patrol over Frenzenberg, his patrol was jumped by British fighters from 57 Squadron, RFC. Heavily outnumbered, Dossenbach was attacked by four fighters and during the ensuing mêlée his aircraft caught fire. It is not certain whether he jumped or fell from the blazing plane, but his remains were returned to the Germans who buried him with full military honours at Frieberg.

## Oberleutnant Eduard Ritter von DOSTLER
(1892–1917)

Eduard Dostler was born on 3 February 1892 in Pottenstein, in Swiss Franconia, the son of a surveyor. After leaving school Dostler joined the 2nd Pioneer Battalion as a cadet and after graduating on 28 October 1912 was commissioned as Leutnant and assigned to the 4th Pioneer Battalion. In 1913, during a military exercise which involved crossing the heavily flooded River Danube, Dostler saved the life of a fellow officer. For this extreme act of bravery he was awarded the Bavarian Life Saving Medal.

At the outbreak of war in August 1914, Dostler's engineering unit was sent to the Front into the thick of the fighting and he was awarded the Iron Cross 2nd Class in the November. In March 1915 he was awarded the Iron Cross 1st Class and the Bavarian Military Service Order 4th Class with Swords. He continued to fight with his battalion until November when he heard that his brother, a pilot, had been killed in action. Dostler then decided that he would apply to be transferred to the German Army Air Service and in February 1916 was posted to *Schutzstaffel* 27. On graduating on 15 June he was posted to *Kampfstaffel* 36 flying Roland C.IIs. With his observer, Leutnant Boes, Dostler carried out reconnaissance missions throughout 1916, but on 17 December 1916 he opened his tally when he shot down a Nieuport Scout whilst carrying out reconnaissance over Verdun.

Ten days later both Dostler and his observer were posted to *Jasta* 13, where they increased their tally by shooting down a Caudron whilst on patrol over Nixeville on 22 January. Early in February they

*Full length shot of an immaculate Oberleutnant Eduard Ritter von Dostler complete with walking stick.*

were posted again, this time to *Jasta* 34, where they stayed until the beginning of June, by which time his tally had risen to eight. Then on 10 June, Dostler was given command of *Jasta* 6. By the end of the following month his score had risen to 21 and he was awarded the Knight's Cross with Swords of the Hohenzollern House Order. This was followed by the award of the *Pour le Mérite*. Dostler's tally contin-

*Oberleutnant Eduard Ritter von Dostler. Leader of Jasta 6, at his Pour le Mérite party. The award around his neck belongs to Manfred von Richthofen (with bandaged head) who placed it around von Dostler's neck.*

ued to mount and by 18 August had reached 26. Then on 21 August, whilst on patrol over the East Roulers area, his good fortune ran out. His patrol was attacked by British RE.8 fighters from 7 Squadron, RFC. Dostler's aircraft was hit several times and he was killed.

He was a sad loss to his *Jasta* as he was a well liked and respected officer. He was posthumously awarded the Bavarian Military Max Joseph Order, making him a Ritter (Knight), the award being back-dated to 18 August.

## Leutnant der Reserve Wilhelm FRANKL
(1893–1917)

The son of a Jewish salesman, Wilhelm Frankl was born on 20 December 1893 in Hamburg. Even at this early time Jewish resentment was festering in Germany and Wilhelm Frankl was to find that obtaining promotion was not going to be easy. After finishing school he joined his father as a salesman, but his sights were set higher than that, quite literally. On 20 July 1913, at the age of 20, Frankl learned to fly at the local flying school and gained his licence. He took part in many competitions, and one in Berlin-Johannisthal resulted in him being awarded his international pilot's licence.

At the outbreak of war in 1914 he applied to join the German Army Air Service and was accepted. Even though he was a qualified pilot, he was trained as an observer and posted to *Feldflieger Abteilung* (FA) 40 in Flanders. He carried out a number of reconnaissance

*Portrait shot of Leutnant Wilhelm Frankl wearing his Pour le Mérite.*

missions during 1914 and was awarded the Iron Cross 2nd Class. During the early part of 1915 there were more reconnaissance missions, and on 10 May 1915 he scored his first victory by shooting down a Voisin with a carbine. For this action he was awarded the Iron Cross 1st Class and later that year was promoted to Vizefeldwebel.

In the autumn of 1915, Frankl applied for training as a fighter pilot and was sent to *Jastaschule* in November 1915. On graduating in the December, he was posted to *Kek* Vaux at the beginning of January 1916, flying Fokker Eindeckers. Within days of arriving he had scored his second victory, another Voisin, whilst on patrol over Woumen. Nine days later he had another Voisin in his sights over the same area and added that one to his tally. By the end of May he had taken his tally to six and had been given a commission as Leutnant. Within a few days he was awarded the Knight's Cross of the Hohenzollern House Order and the Hanseatic Cross. On 10 July Frankl took his score to eight and two days later was given Germany's highest award, the *Pour le Mérite*.

Frankl was posted to *Jasta* 4 on 1 September and by the end of the month had added three more victories to his tally, bringing it up to 13. By the end of 1916 Frankl had only added another two, the year thus finishing on a quiet note for him. Although the beginning of 1917 started quietly, in April things started to happen. On 6 April Frankl claimed four more victims, one of them at night and the

*Leutnant Wilhelm Frankl with the crew of a FE2b of 206 Squadron, RFC, after forcing them to land near Houthem on 2 May 1916. L–R: Captain CEH James (observer); Leutnant Wilhelm Frankl; 2/Lt HCC Aked (pilot).*

remaining three shot down later that same morning, all within the space of one hour. When he scored one more on 7 April it brought his total to 20.

On the afternoon of 8 April 1917, Wilhelm Frankl took off on patrol and flew into a flight of British fighters from 48 Squadron. Heavily outnumbered, his Albatros was badly damaged and was seen to break up in the air, the remains of his aircraft and his body crashing to the ground near Vitry-Sailly. His body was sent back to Germany and Leutnant Wilhelm Frankl was buried with *Albatros D.Va fighter.* full military honours in Berlin-Charlottenburg. In the 1930s the Nazi Party removed his name from the list of air heroes of the First World War because he was Jewish. It was not until 1973 that his name was restored and Luftwaffe Squadron Nr.74 was named after him.

## Oberleutnant Hermann FRICKE

(1890–?)

Hermann Fricke was born on 16 June 1890 at Münster, Westphalia. During the hot German summer of 1912, Hermann Fricke first took to the air as an aircraft passenger from a small airfield near Münster. The 22-year-old immediately realised that this was the element for him and applied to join the German Army Air Service. He was accepted and was assigned to *Feldflieger Abteilung II*. Two years later, on 1 July 1914, he realised his wish to fly as a pilot, and entered the German Flying School at Johannisthal for pilot training. In August 1914 he was awarded his pilot's certificate and rejoined his *Feldflieger Abteilung* unit in September as a reconnaissance pilot.

With the First World War now in progress he was posted, with his unit, to the Western Front and immediately began flying reconnaissance and artillery spotting sorties. Having an interest in photography he began to apply this knowledge to taking aerial photographs of Allied positions. His efforts met with considerable success, which was recognised by the German High Command with the award of the Iron Cross 2nd Class and the Knight's Cross of the Hohenzollern House Order. Wishing to experience what the German infantry was going through on the ground, he asked to be allowed to command an infantry company for a short time. His unusual request was granted and he had a front-line ground command for several weeks. Rejoining his unit he was better able to understand the problems of the German infantry soldier – the principal ones being to get to know the positions of the Allies and the strength of the opposition.

During the battles at the Somme, Arras and Flanders, Fricke flew sortie after sortie taking aerial photographs of the ground struggle beneath his reconnaissance aircraft. Throughout the harsh, muddy winter of 1916–17 the German High Command instructed the now

*Portrait of Oberleutnant Hermann Fricke wearing his Pour le Mérite. Just below his Iron Cross can be seen his observer's badge.*

Oberleutnant Fricke to establish a War Photography Office at their Headquarters. Fricke was appointed to the command of a new unit – Group 2 Series Photography Unit. He equipped his unit's aircraft with 'Reihenbilder' built-in cameras. These cameras were capable of photographing a mile long strip of the ground below, and these were joined together to form an invaluable photographic aerial view of Allied positions. Fricke's aerial photographic maps provided the German High Command with the means to deploy and direct their forces on the ground to good effect.

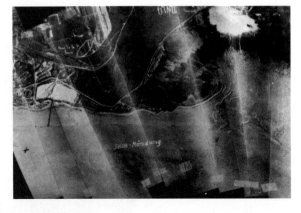

Reihenbilder *or aerial film strips that were attached to each other to form an overall picture. These Reihenbilder show the mouth of the River Seine near Le Havre. At the bottom of the left-hand strip of film can be seen a French coastal airship.*

Oberleutnant Fricke had by now flown well over 160 combat sorties, and his unit had photographed some 3,700 square miles of Allied positions with their aerial cameras. On 23 December 1917 Fricke's innovative aerial photographs gained him the award of the *Pour le Mérite* – for outstanding combat service as both pilot and observer with Fliegerabteilung Nr.2.

Oberleutnant Herman Fricke continued to fly to the end of the First World War and he flew again in the Second World War in the Luftwaffe.

## Leutnant der Reserve Heinrich GONTERMANN
(1896–1917)

Heinrich Gontermann, the son of a cavalry officer, was born on 25 February 1896 in Siegen, Southern Westphalia. After leaving school, Gontermann's future seemed to be destined for the Army, but in August 1914 his future was decided for him. He joined the 6th Uhlan Cavalry Regiment in Hanau and after initial training was sent to the Front where within days of arriving his regiment was in action. The following months were hard, but Heinrich Gontermann's leadership qualities started to show themselves. He was wounded in the September, although not seriously, and was promoted to Feldwebel. Early in the spring of 1915, because of his leadership qualities he was given a field commission as Leutnant and was awarded the Iron Cross 2nd Class. He continued to lead his men throughout 1915, then in October he was transferred to the 80th Fusilier Regiment.

This transfer was not exactly what Heinrich Gontermann wanted.

For some months previously he had been looking at the newly formed German Army Air Service and applied for a transfer to the service. He was accepted and sent for pilot and observer training. On

*Leutnant Heinrich Gontermann leaning against the fuselage of his Albatros wearing the ribbon of the Iron Cross 2nd Class.*

graduation early in 1916, he was posted to *Kampfstaffel* Tergnier as a reconnaissance pilot flying the Roland C.II. In the spring he was posted again, this time to FA 25 where he flew both as a pilot and as an observer on AGO C.Is. After nearly a year of flying reconnaissance missions, Gontermann applied for *Jastaschule* and the transfer to a fighter unit. He was accepted and after graduating on 11 November 1916, was posted to *Jasta* 5. Within three days he had opened his tally by shooting down an FE2b whilst on patrol over Morval.

It was not until March 1917 that Gontermann scored another victory, although not for the want of trying. On 5 March he was awarded the Iron Cross 1st Class, on 6 March he shot down an FE2b of 57 Squadron, RFC, and by the end of the month had raised his tally to six. One month later he had raised it to 17 and been made Staffelführer of *Jasta* 15. Gontermann marked his promotion by shooting down a Spad whilst on patrol over south-east Caronne on 4 May. There was more to celebrate on 6 May, when he was awarded the Knight's Cross with Swords of the

*Portrait of Leutnant Heinrich Gontermann wearing his Pour le Mérite and medal ribbons of the Iron Cross 2nd Class and the Knight's Cross with Swords of the Hohenzollern House Order.*

Hohenzollern House Order. Gontermann showed his appreciation for this on 10 May by shooting down another Spad and a Caudron R4. The following day he shot down another Spad and received the Bavarian Order of Max Josef, and on 14 May he was awarded the ultimate accolade, the *Pour le Mérite*, with his score standing at 21.

From June until the end of September, Gontermann added 17 more victories, bringing his total to 38. Eleven of the 17 victories were observation balloons, four of which were shot down on the evening of 19 August within the space of three minutes of each other. On 2 October 1917 he shot down a Spad whilst on patrol over Laon. Then on 30 October Gontermann took one of the latest Fokker Triplanes that had just been delivered to the *Jasta* up for a test flight. Minutes later, whilst flying above his airfield, the upper wing of the Fokker Triplane suffered structural failure and the aircraft span out of control into the ground. Heinrich Gontermann was pulled from the wreckage still alive, but died from his injuries some hours later. He was just 21 years old.

### Oberleutnant Hermann Wilhelm GÖRING
(1893–1946)

Next to Manfred von Richthofen, the Red Baron, Hermann Göring was probably the most famous, or infamous, German pilot of the First World War. However, it was not for his actions during the First World War that his infamy spread, but rather for his part in the Second World War.

Hermann Göring was born on 12 January 1893 in Rosenheim, Upper Bavaria. He was the son of Heinrich Göring, a very high ranking army officer who had also been a Governor of German South-West Africa. In his early school years Hermann Göring was an unruly, rebellious and undisciplined boy, so his parents looked towards sending him to a military academy. Using a great deal of his influence, Heinrich Göring and a family friend, von Epstein, managed to get Hermann into one of the best military academies at Karlsruhe. From Karlsruhe he progressed to Lichterfelde, an army cadet college for future officers in the German Army. Here college behaviour was based on medieval codes and the cadet society into which Hermann Göring was elected was one that adhered strictly to these codes. In 1912 Hermann Göring graduated from Lichterfelde with brilliant results and was commissioned into the Prinz Wilhelm Regiment Nr.112 and posted to its headquarters at Mühlhausen.

The outbreak of war brought Göring into action within hours of the declaration. This came about because the garrison town of Mühlhausen was situated in Alsace-Lorraine, which had been annexed from the French after the war of 1870, and was on the wrong side of the Rhine. The moment war was declared, the Prinz Wilhelm Regiment retreated across the Rhine onto German territory, whereupon it was moved to the Vosges region, and it was here that Göring contracted rheumatic fever and was hospitalised. Whilst in hospital he was visited by his friend Bruno Loerzer, who had served with Göring in the

*Portrait shot of Hermann Göring taken during the First World War, wearing his* Pour le Mérite.

*Hermann Göring and Bruno Loerzer relaxing in front of Göring's Fokker Triplane.*

regiment but had transferred to the German Army Air Service and become a pilot. Göring reflected on the mud and cold that awaited his return and wrote to his commanding officer requesting a place at the Freiburg flying school. After waiting over two weeks and receiving no reply, Göring obtained the papers and signed them himself, including a transfer paper to the flying school. During this two-week period of the war he had been flying with Loerzer at every opportunity, getting in all the training he could. His transfer was refused and he was ordered to return to his unit which was something Göring had no intention of doing. This situation posed a very serious problem for Hermann Göring as he was open to a charge of desertion and forging papers. He immediately telegraphed his godfather, Ritter von Epstein, who moved in extremely high circles, and suddenly the Crown Prince Friedrich Wilhelm intervened, asking that Göring be posted to the German Fifth Army field air detachment. The charges were miraculously reduced to one of lateness and he was given a medical certificate saying that he was not fit for duty at the Front Line.

In the autumn of 1914, Göring completed his training with FEA 3 as a cameraman-observer, then joined Loerzer at FFA 25. They soon acquired a name for themselves for carrying out the most dangerous of missions and in March received the Iron Cross 2nd Class. Then in May 1915, Göring and Loerzer were sent on one of their most dangerous assignments. They had to carry out a reconnaissance of the fortresses in the Verdun area that were held by the French, and photograph them in detail. Many others had tried but had failed. For

three days Göring and Loerzer flew over the Verdun area and came
back with photographs so detailed that General Erich von Falkenhayn
asked to see them personally. So delighted with the results were the
High Command, that Crown Prince Wilhelm exercised his royal pre-
rogative and invested both Göring and Loerzer with the Iron Cross 1st
Class in the field. In June 1915 Göring was posted to Freiburg for pilot
training, graduating in the October. He was then posted to FA 25 and
on 16 November 1915 he opened his tally by shooting down a
Maurice Farman whilst on patrol over Tahure.

   In 1916 he was posted from one unit to another, first to *Kek*
Stennay flying Fokker E.IIIs, then in March to *Kek* Metz where on 30
July he shot down a Caudron whilst escorting bombers over Memang,
after which he went back to FA 25 on 9 July, and back again to *Kek*
Metz on 7 September. From there he was posted to *Jasta* 7 and a few
weeks later to *Jasta* 5 on 20 October. It was whilst on patrol on 2
November 1916 that he first encountered the British Handley-Page
bomber. As he moved in to look at it he came under fire, which he
returned, killing one of the gunners, but then from out of the clouds
swooped a flight of Sopwith Camels which proceeded to rake his aircraft from stem to stern. As Göring felt the bullets rip into his
fuselage and his thigh, he passed out momentarily then came to as
his aircraft plunged toward the ground. Managing to regain control
of his aircraft, he steered it toward what looked to him like a cemetery just over the German lines. As good fortune would have it, it
turned out to be an emergency hospital, and within a very short time
of crash landing he was on the operating table being repaired.

*Reich Minister Hermann Göring wearing his* Pour le Mérite *and pilot's commemorative badge with his SA uniform.*

*Herman Göring briefing pilots of JG1 prior to leaving on a mission.*

After recuperating Hermann Göring was posted to *Jasta* 26 at the beginning of February, now commanded by his friend Bruno Loerzer. By the end of that month he had raised his tally to six, attracting the attention of the High Command, and increased it further on 10 May when he shot down a DH.4 of 55 Squadron, RFC. One week later he was given command of *Jasta* 27 and by the end of October his total had risen to 15. On 27 October Göring was awarded the Military Karl Friedrich Merit Order, the Knight's Cross with Swords of the Hohenzollern House Order and Knight's Cross 2nd Class with Swords of the Baden Order of the Zähringer Lion. By the end of the year his tally had risen to 16.

In 1918 his total rose steadily and by the end of June it reached 22. At the beginning of June 1918, Göring was awarded Germany's highest award, the *Pour le Mérite*, and on 9 July he was given command of JG1, the Richthofen Squadron, with promotion to Oberleutnant. At this point Hermann decided that his fighting days were over and he did very little combat flying. At the end of the war he was ordered by the German High Command to instruct his pilots to fly their aircraft to an Allied field. Knowing that the Allies just wanted the latest Fokkers, he ordered his pilots to do so, but to set fire to the aircraft the moment they were on the ground. After the war Hermann Göring went to Denmark in a flight advisory capacity, after fighting in the post-war revolution, but returned to Germany in the early 1920s.

Hermann Göring joined the Nazi Party in 1922 and became Adolf Hitler's right-hand man. He progressed through the party as it grew more powerful and took over command of the newly formed Luftwaffe. Göring held a number of other posts throughout the Second World War, but the Luftwaffe was dearest to his heart. During the Second World War he received the Knight's Cross of the Iron Cross and the Grand Cross of the Iron Cross, the only person ever to receive it. He was promoted to Feldmarschall then later to Reichsmarschall, heir apparent to Hitler. Captured by the Americans at the end of the war, Hermann Göring stood trial for war crimes and was convicted. He was sentenced to death by hanging, despite his pleas to be executed by firing squad. In the end he cheated everybody by committing suicide on 15 October 1946, using poison he had been concealing on his person since his capture.

## Oberleutnant Robert Ritter von GREIM
(1892–1945)

Robert Greim, the son of a police captain, was born on 22 June 1892 in Bayreuth, Bavaria. At the age of 14 he became an army cadet until, at the age of 19, on 14 July 1911, he joined the regular army. He was immediately put forward for officer training and on 29 October 1912 joined the Bavarian Field Artillery Regiment. He was commissioned one year later to Leutnant on 25 October 1913. When the war started, Greim's regiment was one of the first in action and he commanded a battery in the Battle of Lorraine at Nancy-Epinal, and on the assaults of St Mihiel and Camp des Romains. For these actions he was awarded the Iron Cross 2nd Class and became the 1st Battalion Adjutant on 15 March 1915. At the end of April 1915, Greim was awarded the Bavarian Military Merit Order 4th Class with Swords.

But like many others he too began to look at the newly formed German Army Air Service and applied for a transfer. Greim began training as an observer on 10 August 1915 and was assigned to FFA 3b where he opened his tally by shooting down a Maurice Farman in October. He was then posted to FA(A) 204 as an observer during the Battle of the Somme, but applied for pilot training toward the end of 1916, and after graduating, was awarded his pilot's certificate and badge. He was then transferred to FA 46b as a reconnaissance pilot on 22 February 1917 and one month later was sent to *Jastaschule* for single-seater training. On completing his conversion training he was

*Portrait shot of Oberleutnant Robert Ritter von Greim wearing his* Pour le Mérite.

posted to *Jasta* 34b on 3 April 1917, flying Albatros D.Vs, Fokker Dr.Is and Fokker D.VIIs. Greim had all his aircraft marked with his own markings of a red cowl, two red fuselage bands and a white silvery tail.

Greim increased his tally on 24 May by shooting down a Spad whilst on patrol over south Mamey and the following day shot down a Caudron R4 over south-east Ramaucourt. At the end of May, he was awarded the Iron Cross 1st Class and the Bavarian Military Merit Order 4th Class with Crown and Swords. By the end of 1917 he had raised his tally to seven, and with it standing at nine, on 29 April 1918, he was awarded the Knight's Cross with Swords of the Hohenzollern House Order. Greim continued to score steadily and on 21 March 1918 was given command of *Jagdgruppe* Nr.10 and later *Jagdgruppe* Nr.9. By the end of October 1918, Greim had raised his tally to 28 and was awarded Germany's highest honour, the *Pour le Mérite*. This was followed almost immediately by the Bavarian Max Joseph Medal, allowing him to put 'Ritter von' in front of Greim, thus making him a 'Knight'. He was also promoted to Oberleutnant. At the end of the war he was with the Bavarian Air Service and later became an adviser to the Chinese Nationalist Air Force.

In the early 1930s Greim became the Director of the Bavarian Sport Flyers Association, then in 1934 he joined the newly formed Luftwaffe with the rank of Major, taking command of the Richthofen Geschwader.

In 1938 he was promoted to the rank of General and during the Second World War commanded Fliegerkorps V, for which he received the Knight's Cross of the Iron Cross on 1 July 1940. On 2 April 1943 he was awarded the Oak Leaves to this medal, followed one year later by the Swords when he was Generaloberst commanding the Air Fleets in Russia. When he was captured by the Americans in 1945 he was in fact Head of the Luftwaffe, a post given to him personally by Adolf Hitler who also promoted him to General Feldmarschall. Greim committed suicide on 24 May 1945 at a hospital in Salzburg, Austria.

## Leutnant der Reserve Wilhelm GRIEBSCH
(1887–1920)

Born in Posen on 30 June 1887. During his school years Griebsch developed an interest in flying which gradually became a passion. At the age of 21 he entered the Technical College in Danzig and four years later – having gained his qualifications as an engineer – he went to Flying School at Berlin-Johannisthal.

He was awarded his pilot's certificate on 29 December 1913, on an Etrich Taube, and set his sights on flying in the newly formed German Army Air Service. When the First World War broke out in 1914 Griebsch immediately volunteered for the Army Air Service, and after initial army officer training left the training school with the rank of Leutnant der Reserve (Territorial Army). Joining *Flieger Abteilung* 250 as a reconnaissance pilot he was immediately in the thick of battle on the Western Front. He then began to fly as an observer with *Flieger-Abteilung* 250, and later with *Flieger Abteilung* 213, where his technical knowledge proved invaluable. His particular spe-

*Leutnant der Reserve Wilhelm Griebsch on the right, with two unknown pilots whilst with FA(A) 213.*

ciality was long range reconnaissance missions of which he completed the enormous total of 345. The outstanding information and technical details obtained by Griebsch proved of great value to the German High Command in their strategic ground battle plans and operations. Even though under enemy air attack he would continue to observe and record the Allied positions far below him, fighting back at the same time with his machine-gun.

His outstanding record of successful patrols as an observer brought him the *Pour le Mérite*, on 30 September 1918. Griebsch was one of the very few observers to be awarded the decoration, most of which were awarded to fighter pilots. Having spent almost four years in the midst of battle he was taken off operational flying and sent back to Berlin to use his hard-won expertise at the Albatros Aircraft Company in Berlin, where he spent the few months remaining of the First World War.

Still with a passion for flying, he obtained work after the war at the Junkers Aircraft

Company in Dessau as a test pilot. On 20 July 1920 Griebsch took off to flight test a new aircraft. With an injured left arm, he was apparently unable to control the aircraft and when at 1,900 feet over Mosigkau, his aircraft fell out of the sky and crashed, killing him instantly.

*Albatros C.III on patrol over the Belgian Front.*

## Oberleutnant Jürgen von GRONE
(1887–?)

The youngest son of army officer Oberleutnant Otto von Grone, Jürgen was born at Schwerin on 14 November 1887. After leaving school he entered college to study law and political sciences. Toward the end of his studies von Grone volunteered for a one year enlistment with the 1st Guard Field Artillery Regiment.

When the First World War began von Grone was a Leutnant serving with the 11 Field Artillery Regiment on the Western Front. His unit was involved in heavy fighting in the Namur sector of the front and the battle experience gained was to be put to good use by von Grone later when he became an observer. He was posted to the Eastern Front in 1915 and during heavy fighting was wounded and hospitalised. On returning to duty he became commander of one of the new mobile anti-aircraft trains the Germans were using. He was awarded the Iron Cross 2nd Class, followed soon after by the Iron Cross 1st Class.

In December 1915 he applied for transfer to the Air Service as an observer and was accepted. After completing his training he was posted to *Flieger Abteilung* 222 where his specialist task as a reconnaissance observer was to photograph Allied troop movements and positions. By the summer of 1917 he had flown 130 reconnaissance missions and was promoted to command the Photography Troop of the German 7th Army. On 10 September 1917 he was the first observer to photograph Paris from a height of 7,000 metres.

*Oberleutnant Jürgen von Grone speaking with General von Emmich whilst the General was on a visit to FA 222.*

On 13 October 1918 Oberleutnant Jürgen von Grone was awarded the *Pour le Mérite* for his outstanding contribution to the war effort. Part of his citation read:

> Oberleutnant von Grone performed outstanding deeds during the large battles of 7th Army. Since the end of May he has made 50 long range missions over enemy territory. The results of this long range reconnaissance – up to 100 kilometres behind enemy lines – contributed substantially to our knowledge of

enemy positions. Leutnant von Grone carried out numerous long range flights, among them twelve over 100 kilometres behind the enemy front, despite enemy defences, up to 6,000 metres altitude under heavy air attack he prevailed. By reason of his above average performance I consider him worthy of the award of the *Pour le Mérite*.


Signed: Hugo Sperrle,
         Hauptmann,
         Commandant of Flyers, 7th Army.


[Sperrle later became a Second World War Field Marshal].

Von Grone survived the First World War and was discharged from the Army in 1920 with the rank of Hauptmann.


### General der Kavallerie Ernst von HOEPPNER
(1860-1922)

Born in Tonnin on the Pomerian island of Wollin on 14 June 1860, Ernst Hoeppner appeared to be destined for a military career from a very early age. On finishing his schooling, he joined the Army as a cadet. On graduating, he was promoted to Leutnant and assigned to Dragoon Regiment Nr.6 stationed at Stendal. In 1890 he was posted to the War Academy, and upon graduating in 1893 was promoted to Oberleutnant and assigned the post of Squadron Commander of Dragoon Regiment Nr.14 in Colmar, Alsace. An appointment to the General Staff in 1902 heralded the start of a distinguished career. This was followed two years later by promotion to Major and a staff officer's position with the 9th Army Corps at Altona. In 1906 Hoeppner was promoted to Oberstleutnant and given command of the Husaren-Regiment Nr.13 stationed in Diedenhofen.

Oberstleutnant Hoeppner's organisational capabilities soon came to the fore, and these were rewarded in 1908 by his appointment to Chief of the General Staff of the 7th Army Corps. This position was to last until 1912 when he was given command of the 4th Cavalry Brigade in Bromberg, one of the most prestigious commands in the

*Portrait shot of General der Kavallerie Ernst von Hoeppner wearing his* Pour le Mérite.

German Army. This was culminated in 1913, when the title of 'von' was bestowed upon him, giving him the right to change his name to Ernst von Hoeppner, making him a Teutonic Knight.

At the outbreak of war in 1914, von Hoeppner was Chief of the General Staff of the 3rd Army, a position he was to hold until May 1915 when he took over command of the 14th Reserve Division of the 1st Army. Such was the rapid movement of senior officers at the time, as the Army attempted to stabilise its organisational problems, that von Hoeppner was appointed Chief of the General Staff of the 2nd Army within a few months. In June 1916 he was moved again

*L–R: Oberst Leith-Thomsen, Manfred von Richthofen and General der Kavallerie Ernst von Hoeppner. The photograph was taken whilst Manfred von Richthofen was on a visit to Berlin.*

when he took over command of the 75th Reserve Division. Again the German High Command could not make up its mind, when they recalled von Hoeppner from the Eastern Front late in June 1916. He was in a desperate situation at the time with superior Russian forces threatening to break the German defences at Lake Naroch. An earlier attempt to break the defences had failed, but now they had been breached, with the Austro-Hungarian 4th Army (under the command of the incompetent Archduke Joseph Ferdinand) being virtually destroyed.

In October 1916 von Hoeppner was promoted to General and appointed Kommandierender General of the German Army Air Service. He immediately set to work to unify all the various units under one command structure. Because the German Air Force had started life as 'general units' consisting of six or less aircraft, its development had been ragged, with specialised units coming in under the command of various structures. Now there were single-seater fighters, single-seater reconnaissance, single-seater artillery liaison, escort fighters and bombers, all needing to come under one command structure. Von Hoeppner set about it with a single-minded purposefulness and by the spring of 1917 had unified the entire German Army Air Service.

On 8 April 1917, the German High Command recognised General Ernst von Hoeppner's achievement by awarding him Germany's highest award, the *Pour le Mérite*. He was to stay at his post until the end of the war, when he retired to his home on the island of Wollin, where he died on 25 September 1922 at the age of 62.

### Leutnant der Reserve Walter HÖHNDORF
(1892–1917)

Walter Höhndorf, the son of a schoolteacher, was born in Prutzke, Bavaria, on 10 November 1892. He was an extremely bright schoolboy who enjoyed a passion for anything mechanical. On leaving school he went to Paris to study motor and engineering mechanics, and whilst there, in September 1913, learned to fly and received his civilian pilot's certificate No.582 on 3 November 1913.

Höhndorf returned to Germany, took part in many air displays, became one of the best aerobatic pilots in the country and carried out aerobatic manoeuvres never seen before. He then turned his hand to designing, and helped with the production of aircraft with the *Union Flugzeugwerke* at Teltow. At the outbreak of war in 1914 Höhndorf immediately volunteered for the German Army Air Service, gaining a commission as Leutnant on 15 March 1915. Because of his vast flying experience, albeit crammed into a relatively short time, he was assigned to Siemens-Schuckert, the aircraft manufacturer, as a test pilot on their large aircraft. After nearly a year of test flying Höhndorf applied for fighter pilot training and was sent to *Jastaschule*. On graduating he was sent to FA 12 and later to FA 67 as a reconnaissance pilot where he was awarded the Iron Cross 2nd Class. At the beginning of January 1917 he was posted to FA 12 again where, on 17 January, he claimed his first victory when he shot down a French Voisin from *Escadrille* VB.105

*Portrait of Leutnant Walter Höhndorf wearing his* Pour le Mérite.

whilst on patrol in the Alsace region. Two days later he shot down another Voisin from *Escadrille* VB.101 over Medevich.

Walter Höhndorf was then posted to *Kek* Vaux of FA 23 at the beginning of April 1916, flying Fokker S.VIIIs, and claimed his 3rd victim, a Nieuport, on 10 April. The award of the Iron Cross 1st Class and the Knight's Cross with Swords of the Hohenzollern House Order came at the beginning of June, followed at the end of July by the *Pour le Mérite*, at which time his tally stood at 11. At the beginning of August he was posted to *Jasta* 1, then to *Jasta* 4, but it was decided that his experience in testing aircraft was just as valuable as his experience as a fighter pilot. He returned to test pilot duties and instructing at Valenciennes for a short period, but then on 15 August 1917, was given command of *Jasta* 14 on the Western Front. His command was to be short lived. At the beginning of September 1917 he returned to Valenciennes to test an AEG DI, No. 4400/17, an aircraft he had helped to design. During the test flight he experienced problems, crashed whilst attempting to land at Ire-le-Sec and died from his injuries almost immediately.

### Oberleutnant Erich HOMBURG
(1886–?)

The son of a forester, Erich Homburg was born on 2 October 1886 in Rosenthal, Bavaria. After leaving school, he joined the Army as a cadet with Reserve Field Artillery Regiment Nr.12. When war broke out in August 1914, Homburg had already been awarded a commission and was the regiment's ordnance officer as well as the unit adjutant. The regiment moved to the Western Front and almost immediately was involved in the conflict. After many months of intense and heavy fighting, Homburg was later awarded the Iron Cross 2nd Class.

*Portrait shot of Oberleutnant Erich Homburg wearing his Pour le Mérite, Iron Cross 1st Class and his observer's badge.*

During a lull in the early part of 1915, Homburg was offered a flight in a reconnaissance aircraft. He was so taken with the flight and the relative freedom it afforded that he applied for a transfer to the German Army Air Service. In the spring of 1915 he was accepted and posted for flying training. On graduating in the autumn, Homburg was posted to Field Flying Unit 34 as a reconnaissance pilot. He quickly developed an interest in communications and was assigned the post of communications officer. On 25 September 1915 he was awarded the Iron Cross 1st Class for his reconnaissance work. During the next two years he created a reporting system that used ground-to-air radio, and became the first flyer to use it. During this time he also turned his attention and skills to aerial photography and carried out flight strip photographic reconnaissance missions over the Battles of the Somme, Verdun, Champagne and Romania. During the German offensive in Italy Homburg was sent to carry out aerial photographic missions, which greatly helped the campaign. At the beginning of August 1918 he returned to the

Western Front and was given command of Army Flight Unit 260. On 13 October Homburg was awarded Germany's highest honour, the *Pour le Mérite*, one of the very few non-fighter pilots to receive the award. He was also promoted to Oberleutnant in recognition of the 239 tactical reconnaissance and photographic missions he had flown over enemy territory.

When Germany finally capitulated in 1918, Homburg managed to get every single one of his aircraft, every piece of equipment and all his personnel back into Germany.

He continued with his interest in aerial photography using the expertise he had gained during the war for peaceful purposes. The planning of new airfields for commercial use was one of the applications for which aerial photography was used. He was appointed Director of Air Transport-AG for Lower Saxony in 1926, at Hannover's city airport administration, and in the early 1930s Homburg was appointed President of the Reich's Association of Regional Air Traffic Companies. He was also president of a number of sporting flying organisations, including Director of the Aviation Office in Hamburg.

At the onset of the Second World War, Homburg returned to active service with the Luftwaffe, attaining the rank of Generalmajor on 1 November 1940.

## Oberleutnant Hans-Georg HORN
(1892–?)

Born on 28 April 1892, in the small town of Berbisdorf in Silesia, Hans-Georg Horn was the son of the local Lutheran pastor. After finishing his schooling Hans-Georg Horn attended the military school at Danzig as a cadet. At the outbreak of war in 1914, whilst holding the rank of Unteroffizier at the college, he was sent to the infantry regiment that was his parent unit. The regiment was moved to the Western Front and within days of arriving they were in action. On 8 August 1914 Horn was involved in the storming of Maas Heights during the Battle of Longwy. One month later he was involved in the Battle of Combres where his leadership during the battle earned him promotion to Leutnant and the Iron Cross 2nd Class.

On 17 July 1915, whilst leading his troops at the front, Horn was wounded during an assault on enemy positions. He returned to his unit after a week in hospital, but at the end of July was wounded

Leutnant Horn

*Portrait of Oberleutnant Hans-Georg Horn wearing his Pour le Mérite and the medal ribbon of the Knight's Cross with Swords of the Hohenzollern House Order.*

again, this time badly. Whilst in hospital he was awarded the Iron Cross 1st Class, but a chance meeting with a pilot from the German Army Air Service was to change his whole attitude to the war. At the end of October, just after being released from hospital, Hans-Georg Horn applied for transfer to the German Army Air Service and was accepted. He was posted to Flying Reserve Unit 10 on 5 December 1915 for training as an observer. On graduating in February 1916, Horn was posted to a defence squadron flying reconnaissance missions for the infantry. The remaining year was spent flying sortie after sortie, then in January 1917 he was posted to Defence Squadron 11 for two months, then to *Kagohl* 221 in the April.

The move to *Kagohl* 221 was to bring Horn into contact with some of the most intensive fighting of the war, including the battles at Verdun. He and his pilot, Otto Jahnke, flew almost daily and this was recognised by the German High Command on 15 July 1917, when he was awarded the Knight's Cross with Swords of the Hohenzollern House Order. It was known that Horn was, without doubt, one of the best observers in the German Army Air Service, and this was borne out in November 1917, when, during the battles near Geluveld, Horn and his pilot flew six flights in the most horrendous weather conditions. The information they brought back enabled the infantry on the ground to make important advances whilst saving the lives of many of their troops.

On 23 December 1917 Hans-Georg Horn was awarded the *Pour le Mérite*, whilst his pilot Otto Jahnke received the Military Merit Cross, making Horn one of only five observers to be honoured with the *Pour le Mérite*. In May 1918 he was posted to the 7th Infantry Division as a flying liaison officer for two months with the rank of Oberleutnant. He returned to his unit in August and was wounded later the same month, which seemingly ended his active flying career. At the end of the war, he had over 300 sorties over enemy territory to his name. His flying days were not quite over, for with the signing of the Armistice he was assigned to *Kagohl* 401, flying reconnaissance missions for the border police. In November 1919 Hans-Georg Horn resigned from the Army and returned to civilian life.

## Oberleutnant Max IMMELMANN
(1890–1916)

The son of a wealthy factory owner in Dresden, Max Immelmann was born on 21 September 1890. Seven years later his father died of tuberculosis leaving Max to determine his own future. Being no

*Portrait shot of Oberleutnant Max Immelmann wearing his Pour le Mérite. On his left breast are the medals: Saxon Commander's Cross to the Military St Heinrich's Order 2nd Class; the Knight's Cross with Swords of the Hohenzollern House Order; Knight's Cross to the Military St Heinrich's Order; Saxon Albert Order 2nd Class with Swords; Saxon Friedrich August Medal in Silver and the Bavarian Military Merit Order 4th Class with Swords.*

*Oberleutnant Max Immelmann in the cockpit of his Fokker Eindecker.*

academic, at the age of 15 he was sent to the Dresden Cadet School. After completing the course, he joined Railway Regiment Nr.2 in Berlin-Schöneberg with the rank of Fähnrich. He was assigned to the War Academy at Anklam and upon graduating Immelmann applied for leave of absence to go to the Engineering School at Dresden to study machine building. His studies were cut short with the outbreak of the First World War and he was returned to his regiment and was immediately assigned to Railway Regiment Nr.1.

However, since his youth, his main interest had been in anything mechanical, so he applied for a transfer to the German Army Air Service, which was approved and he was posted in November 1914 for basic flying training at the school in Johannisthal, Berlin. On completion of his initial training he was posted to Aldershof for advanced training before being awarded his pilot's badge and certificate. In February 1915 Immelmann was posted to FFA 62 (later to become *Kek* Douai) flying LVG two-seaters on observation and escort patrols. With him on these patrols was another recently qualified pilot by the name of Oswald Boelcke, and within a few months they had established for themselves a reputation as top scouting pilots.

In May 1915 Immelmann was moved from the LVGs to the unit's single-seat fighter, the Fokker Eindecker. On 1 August he won his first victory, a BE2c of 2 Squadron, RFC. By the end of September his tally had risen to three confirmed plus two possibles, and the award of the Iron Cross 2nd Class. October and November brought another four victories and promotion to Oberleutnant, the Iron Cross 1st Class and the Knight's Cross with Swords of the Hohenzollern House Order. On 12 January 1916 Max Immelmann, or the 'Eagle of Lille' as he has become known, was awarded the coveted *Pour le Mérite*. His tally rose to 13 by the end of March and more awards were given to him: the Saxon Commander's Cross to the Military St Heinrich's Order 2nd Class; the Knight's Cross to the Military St Heinrich's Order; the Saxon Albert Order 2nd Class with Swords; the Saxon Friedrich August Medal in Silver and the Bavarian Military Merit Order 4th Class with Swords.

On 18 June 1916 he was engaged in a fight with FE2bs of 25 Squadron in his Fokker (246/16). Twisting and turning around in the packed skies, he suddenly came under fire from an FE2b flown by Captain G R McGubbin together with his gunner, Corporal J H Waller. Their report states that they shot the Fokker's propeller away causing the engine to tear loose from its mountings, sending the aircraft plunging to the ground. The German High Command, however, saddened by the loss of one of its most decorated and promising fighter pilots, announced that Immelmann had died because of a defective synchronised gear in the gun. This, they claimed, had caused Immelmann, whilst engaged by overwhelming enemy odds, to shoot off his own propeller with the result that the torque on the engine caused it to be ripped from its mountings, plunging Max Immelmann to his death.

Max Immelmann's skill as a pilot was greatly respected by the British and on the day of his funeral they flew a special sortie over the spot where he was killed and dropped a wreath. The black funeral sash around it read:

In memory of Oberleutnant Immelmann, our brave and knightly opponent, from the British Royal Flying Corps.

*The twisted wreckage of Max Immelmann's aircraft minutes after it had crashed.*

### Leutnant Josef Carl Peter JACOBS
(1894–1978)

The son of a middle class businessman, Josef Jacobs was born in Kreuzkapelle, Rhineland, on 15 May 1894. His interest in all things mechanical showed itself in 1912 when, at the age of 18, he learned to fly. Two years later at the outbreak of the First World War, Josef Jacobs enlisted in the German Army Air Service and was posted to FEA 9 to be trained as a military pilot. On graduating he was posted to FA 11 as a reconnaissance pilot, and for over a year was engaged in missions over the lines. Early in 1916 he was posted to Fokker *Staffel* West flying Fokker E IIIs. He opened his tally unofficially on 1 February when he claimed a Caudron, but it was unconfirmed. The end of March brought a claim for a balloon, for which he was awarded the Iron Cross 2nd Class, but it was not the victory Jacobs wanted for his *Ehrenbecher* (Honour Cup); he wanted a 'Knight's' victory, not the shooting down of a stationary object in the sky.

On 25 October 1916 Jacobs was posted to *Jasta* 22 at the request of its commander, Oberleutnant Erich Honemanns, a long-time friend. Within weeks of his arriving at *Jasta* 22 he was posted temporarily to *Jastaschule* 1 as an instructor, where he spent part of the winter. Returning to *Jasta* 22 at the end of January 1917, he was awarded the Iron Cross 1st Class which he celebrated by opening his tally with the squadron by shooting down a Caudron R4 whilst on patrol over Terny Sorny on 23 January. By the end of August his tally had risen to five and he was appointed commander of *Jasta* 7. With the appointment came the award of the Knight's Cross with Swords of the Hohenzollern House Order. By the end of 1917 Jacobs' tally had risen to 12 and his *Jasta* was re-equipped with Fokker Triplanes. Jacobs had his aircraft painted all black and it was soon to become instantly recognisable by Allied airmen.

The beginning of 1918 was quiet for *Jasta* 7. There was a lull in hostilities and Jacobs used the time to work his *Jasta* into a fighting unit,

*Portrait of Leutnant Josef Carl Peter Jacobs wearing his* Pour le Mérite.

Unser erfolgreicher Kampfflieger
Leutnant Jacobs

but this did not last long and in April Jacobs claimed his next victim, an RE8 of 7 Squadron, RFC, over west Ostend. The fighting became intense and by the end of July, after surviving a mid-air collision with another Fokker Triplane, Jacobs' tally had risen to 24 and he was awarded Germany's most prestigious award, the *Pour le Mérite*. He gradually became Germany's greatest exponent of the Fokker Triplane and by the end of 1918 had disposed of 48 of the Allies' aircraft. Even after the Armistice he, along with Osterkamp and Sachsenberg, fought against the communists in the Baltic.

In the early 1920s Jacobs became a flight instructor with the Turkish Army, helping them develop quite a formidable air force. In 1931 he became a director of the Adler works, still maintaining his interest in aviation. Two years later he set up his own aircraft manufacturing plant at Erfurt although this was not a great success. Speed was still a passion and he became involved in the world of car and powerboat racing and bobsledding. Prior to the start of the Second World War, Jacobs did not volunteer for the newly formed Luftwaffe but at the onset was commissioned as a Major in the reserves. He was a reluctant officer in the Luftwaffe and his views on the National Socialist Party were well known and documented. At one point he even moved his company away from Germany to Holland in order to prevent Göring becoming a major shareholder. At the end of the war Josef Jacobs moved away from aviation and started a crane operating company, but such was his love of aviation that he became one of the greatest sources of historical information on German First World War aviation and personnel.

*Leutnant Josef Jacobs' Ehrenbecher (Honour Cup) made for him to commemorate his first victory.*

*Leutnant Jacobs with his ground crew in front of his Fokker E.III.*

*Rare photograph of an RE8 from No. 9 Squadron being shot down over Hamel whilst carrying out ammunition drops.*

## Hauptmann Alfred KELLER
(1882–1974)

The son of a tax collector, Alfred Keller was born on 19 September 1882 in Bochum, Westphalia. On leaving school in 1897 Keller entered the army as a cadet, and on graduating in 1902 was assigned to Pioneer Battalion Nr.17 stationed at Thorn. In 1903 he was commissioned as a Leutnant, but it would be a further nine years before he was promoted to Oberleutnant. In the autumn of 1912 Keller applied for transfer to the newly formed German Army Air Service, and was accepted. He was posted to Metz for training as an observer and on completion of the course, he reapplied for training as a pilot. He was posted to flying school at Niederneuendorf in the spring of 1913 and upon graduating was posted to the flying station at Darmstadt.

On the outbreak of war in August 1914, Keller was posted to the Western Front in command of *Kagohl* 27 and promoted to Hauptmann. He carried out a number of reconnaissance missions during the first year, among which was a reconnaissance flight in October 1914 over Paris. This was the cause of great concern to Parisians, as up to that point they thought that hostilities were well away from them and offered no direct threat. What it did do was to reveal the vulnerability of the city to its inhabitants and Keller was awarded the Iron Cross 2nd Class for this sortie. In 1915 Keller was given command of AFP 5 and saw extensive action in reconnaissance and scouting missions in the areas of the Somme and Verdun. In September 1915 he was given command of *Kagohl* 40 until the autumn of 1916 when he was asked to command Night Flying Unit 1, which brought a new concept to the war. Keller developed this unit until 1 April 1917, when he was given command of *Bogohl* 1 and awarded the Iron Cross 1st Class for his work in this field.

*Bogohl* 1 was the first official bombing squadron to carry out night bombing attacks, and from then until the end of the war, Keller and his bomber crews carried out numerous missions, including one in September 1917 on Dunkirk which forced the British to retreat to the safety of Calais. Over 100,000 kilograms of bombs were dropped on Dunkirk, causing a large number of casualties and considerable damage. For this, Keller was awarded the Knight's Cross with Swords of the Hohenzollern House Order, and then, on 4 December, he was awarded Germany's highest award, the *Pour le Mérite*.

Keller continued his night bombing attacks, and on the night of 30/31 January 1918 he led a surprise attack on Paris, causing great consternation and panic. Although the ground artillery put up a defence of sorts, his entire squadron returned without a scratch. Keller continued his attacks on the city, with the result that vital artillery pieces had to be moved from the front to help defend the

*Portrait of Hauptmann Alfred Keller wearing his Pour le Mérite and the medal ribbons of the Iron Cross 2nd Class and the Knight's cross with Swords of the Hohenzollern House Order*

*Alfred Keller as Oberleutnant (left foreground) talking to Hauptmann Oswald Boelcke.*

*Fokker Dr.1, No. 102/17, in which Kurt Wolff was later shot down and killed by Sub Lieutenant N M MacGregor of 10(N) Squadron, on 15 September 1917.*

capital. At the end of the war Keller left the German Army Air Service and became the head of the German *Luftreederei*, which was involved in airship transport.

In the early 1930s Hermann Göring approached Keller and asked him for help in developing the new German Luftwaffe. Keller joined the Luftwaffe in 1935 with the rank of Oberst, and was given command of *Bogohl* 154. He was promoted to the rank of Generalmajor in April 1936, then to Generalleutnant on 1 February 1938 and given the post of Commanding General of the East Prussian Luftwaffe. Keller held the post for a year, after which he was given command of the 4th Air Division HQ, Brunswick. On 24 June 1940 he was awarded the Knight's Cross of the Iron Cross (the award made him the recipient of Germany's highest awards for valour in both the First World War and the Second World War) and promoted to Generaloberst. This was followed by the appointment to Commander-in-Chief of Luftflotte I in Berlin and the Russian Front. At the end of the war Keller was Commanding Officer of the Luftwaffe Anti-Tank Service. He died in Berlin on 11 February 1974 at the age of 92.

## Leutnant Hans KIRSCHSTEIN
(1896–1918)

Leutnant Hans Kirschstein was born in Koblenz on 5 August 1896. At the outbreak of war he joined the 3rd Pioneer Battalion and was soon in action, first in Poland, then in France. In the spring of 1915 his battalion was shipped to Galicia, Macedonia, and it was here that Kirschstein contracted malaria. He was shipped back to Germany for treatment and convalescence, returning to Galicia in the December. It was while in hospital that Kirschstein started to make enquiries about the newly formed German Army Air Service. In February 1916 he applied for transfer to aviation and was accepted. At the beginning of May he was posted to the flying school at Schliessheim, and after graduating was posted to bomber squadron FA 19. During the battles in Flanders he became notorious amongst the Allies for his low-level strafing runs on tanks. He was also one of the first pilots to carry out a bombing raid on Dover, for which he received the Iron Cross 2nd Class.

During 1917 Kirschstein flew with FA 256 and FA 3, building his reputation as he went along. Then at the beginning of February 1918 he asked to be posted to a fighter squadron and was sent to *Jastaschule* for conversion training. On 13 March 1918, after graduating, he was posted to *Jasta* 6, the Richthofen Circus. Within five days he had opened his tally by shooting down a Sopwith Camel from 54 Squadron, RFC, on 18 March, and by the end of the month had raised it to three. He received the Iron Cross 1st Class in May, followed by the Knight's Cross with Swords of the Hohenzollern House Order.

On 10 June Kirschstein took over command of *Jasta* 6 with his tally at 24. By the end of June 1918 Kirschstein had raised his tally to 27,

A group of the top German fighter aces of the First World War, L–R: Oberleutnant Bruno Loerzer; Oberleutnant Hermann Göring; Oberleutnant Lothar von Richthofen; Leutnant Hans Kirschstein; Leutnant Kreft (Tech. Officer); Leutnant von Malinckrodt and Leutnant Schubert.

and on 24 June 1918 he was awarded the *Pour le Mérite*. But his delight was to be short lived. A month later, on 11 July, Kirschstein took his personal Fokker to the Aircraft Park at Fismes for its annual complete overhaul. With him, flying a Hannover CL.II, was a new pilot, Leutnant Johannes Markgraf, who had joined *Jasta* 6 one week previously and who was to fly Kirschstein back to the squadron. Just after taking off on the return flight the Hannover crashed, killing both men instantly. It was revealed later, at a board of inquiry, that Markgraf had never flown a Hannover before, and as nothing else appeared to contribute to the crash, it was deemed to be pilot error.

*Otto Kissenberth wearing his Pour le Mérite. Note the glasses worn by Kissenberth, one of only three German pilots to wear glasses during the First World War.*

## Oberleutnant Otto KISSENBERTH
(1893–1919)

Otto Kissenberth was born on 26 February 1893 in Landshut, Bavaria, the son of a local businessman. It was obvious from the start that his interests were in engineering and after his initial schooling he was sent to study engineering at Grenoble University in France, then on to technical college in Munich to complete his degree in mechanical engineering. After graduation Kissenberth went to work for the Gustav Otto Aircraft Works where he took a diploma in aircraft engineering.

At the outbreak of war Kissenberth volunteered for the newly formed German Army Air Service as a pilot. He was posted to FEA.1 at Schliessheim for training where, after graduating, he was awarded his pilot's certificate and badge and posted to FA 8b as a reconnaissance pilot in October 1914. Early in March 1915 he was promoted to Vizefeldwebel, but on 21 March, whilst on a reconnaissance patrol over the Vosges Mountains, he was attacked by Allied fighters. Although seriously wounded he managed to get his aircraft back to base. The injuries put him into hospital for over three months, and when he had recovered he was posted on 8 July to FA 9b which was based in Toblach in the Dolomites.

His first mission with the squadron was a long range bombing raid on Cortina on 31 July 1915. The raid was a complete success and Kissenberth's status amongst his fellow pilots rose dramatically. Not long afterwards the squadron was moved from Italy to the comparatively quiet front in the Vosges Mountains. The lack of action soon prompted Otto Kissenberth to apply for fighter pilot training and in the early part of 1916 he was accepted and posted to *Jastsachule*. A number of other reconnaissance pilots from FA 9b had also requested single-seater pilot training and on completion all were posted to *Kek* Einsisheim which had grown out of FA 9b.

There followed a number of uneventful months until on 12 October 1916, whilst on a bombing raid on Oberdorf (a raid which was later to become famous), Kissenberth shot down three Allied aircraft – two Maurice Farmans from *Escadrille* F.123 and a Breguet V from No.3 Naval Wing, RNAS. This was even more remarkable considering Kissenberth wore glasses, something virtually unheard of in fighter pilot circles. For his major part in the raid Kissenberth was awarded the Iron Cross 2nd Class and commissioned Leutnant.

*Oberleutnant Otto Kissenberth, of Jasta 23, standing in front of a captured Sopwith Camel which subsequently became his own. He was later seriously injured in a crash in this aircraft.*

The German air force was expanding and *Kek* Einsisheim formed part of a new *Jasta, Jasta* 16. By the beginning of July Kissenberth's tally had risen to six, then on 4 August he was made commander of *Jasta* 23. He was awarded the Iron Cross 1st Class later the same month and continued to increase his tally steadily in his Albatros D.V with his personal insignia, a white and yellow edelweiss, on the fuselage. On 2 October 1917 Kissenberth scored his 18th victory and was awarded the Bavarian Military Merit Order 4th Class with Crown and Swords on 5 December.

On 29 May 1918, with his tally standing at 20, Kissenberth was flying a captured Sopwith Camel, with which he had scored his last victory, when he crashed on landing and was severely injured. So bad were the injuries that he was told that he would not be fit enough to fly again. Whilst in hospital he was awarded the Knight's Cross of the Hohenzollern House Order and on 24 July the *Pour le*

*Mérite.* On 19 August, just two days after being discharged from the hospital, Kissenberth was promoted to Oberleutnant and made commandant of the Schliessheim Flying School, where he stayed until the end of the war. He died whilst mountaineering in the Bavarian Alps in 1919.

*Portrait of Oberleutnant Hans Klein wearing his* Pour le Mérite. *He is also wearing the medal ribbons of the Iron Cross 2nd Class and the Knight's Cross with Swords of the Hohenzollern House Order.*

## Oberleutnant der Reserve Hans KLEIN
(1891–1944)

Hans Klein was born in Stetin, Bavaria, on 17 January 1891. His childhood, like many others at that time, was uneventful but this was to change in August 1914 at the outbreak of the First World War. Hans Klein volunteered for the Army and after initial training with the 34th Infantry Regiment was sent to the Western Front. Almost immediately he was in action and his leadership qualities were rewarded by rapid promotion, first to Unteroffizier then to Feldwebel; he was also awarded the Iron Cross 2nd Class. In March 1915, just six months after volunteering, Hans Klein was given a field commission as Leutnant. He continued to fight on the Western Front and by the end of the year had been awarded the Iron Cross 1st Class. Toward the end of 1915, Leutnant Hans Klein applied for transfer to the German Army Air Service and was accepted.

In the spring of 1916 Klein began his pilot training, and graduated in July. He was posted to a *Kek* where he was immediately in action. On 20 August he was involved in a dogfight with Allied fighters and claimed to have shot down a BE2c, but it was unconfirmed. He was then posted to *Jasta* 4 in November, where he underwent intensive fighter training. It was put to good effect, as on 4, 7, 8, 11, 13 and 30 April 1917 he claimed eight victories – all confirmed. The one on 8 April was unique inasmuch as it was the first night-fighter victory of the war. On 13 July, with his tally standing at 16, Hans Klein was wounded in a

*Albatros aircraft of Jasta 10 at Cortrai.*

dogfight with 20 Squadron, RFC. He managed to return to base but was hospitalised. On his return to *Jasta* 4 at the end of August he was awarded the Knight's Cross with Swords of the Hohenzollern House Order and given command of *Jasta* 10. He took over command of *Jasta* 10 on 27 September and continued to raise his tally which by the end of November stood at 22 and he was awarded Germany's most prestigious award, the *Pour le Mérite*.

The beginning of 1918 saw Hans Klein promoted to Oberleutnant, but on 19 February he encountered an Allied patrol and after a vicious dogfight he was wounded again. This time he lost his right thumb which, in essence, ended his combat flying career and he served out the rest of the war as a ground officer with *Jasta* 10.

With the signing of the Armistice, Hans Klein went back to school and gained an engineering degree. After spending the following years in engineering, he was enticed back into the newly formed Luftwaffe in 1935 and given the rank of Major. From October 1939 to January 1940 he commanded JG 53, before being promoted to Oberst and given the command of a fighter area. In 1942 he was promoted to Generalmajor and became Deputy Commander of all Luftwaffe fighters. He died on 18 November 1944.

## Kapitänleutnant Rudolf KLEINE

(1886–1917)

Rudolf Kleine was born on 28 August 1886 at Minden, Westphalia. His father was an infantry Colonel in the Infantry Regiment Nr.15, so it was no surprise that Rudolf Kleine wanted to join the Army after leaving school. He joined the Corps of Cadets in 1901 and graduated as a Leutnant on 14 June 1905. He was assigned to Infantry Regiment

Hauptmann Kleine

*Informal portrait of Rudolf Kleine as a Hauptmann wearing the medal ribbons of the Iron Cross 2nd Class and the Knight's Cross with Swords of the Hohenzollern House Order.*

Nr.65, where he made rapid progress, becoming the battalion adjutant in 1910. In the spring of 1913 Rudolf Kleine decided that the infantry was losing its appeal, applied for transfer to the German Army Air Service and was accepted.

In September 1913 Kleine was sent to the Herzog-Karl-Eduard Flying School at Gotha for training as a pilot and upon graduating in June 1914 was awarded his oval silver pilot's badge and assigned to Air Battalion No.3 at Cologne. In August 1914 he participated in one of the first battles of the war when he flew reconnaissance sorties for the German brigades which had been charged with capturing the fortress city of Liège. For his part in the action Kleine was awarded the Iron Cross 2nd Class and promoted to Oberleutnant. For the next year Kleine carried out numerous reconnaissance missions over enemy lines, bringing back important information. On one of these, in July 1915, he was wounded in the arm and hospitalised. After recovering he was promoted to Hauptmann and in the December was posted to Ostend, Belgium, to take command of *Kagohl* 1. His appearance as commander of *Kagohl* 1, wearing the oval silver badge of a qualified German military pilot, was an unusual sight amongst *Kagohl* commanders as nearly all of them were observers.

For the next 12 months his squadron made numerous scouting and reconnaissance missions over enemy lines, including one crucial one carried out by Kleine himself when he reported the massing of French troops for the battle of Champagne. The precise report given by Kleine helped the German infantry prepare for the assault, thus cutting their losses. For his part in this, Kleine was awarded the Knight's Cross with Swords of the Hohenzollern House Order and the Iron Cross 1st Class. On 23 August 1916, Kleine was given command of Field Flying Unit 53, a position he held until 23 June 1917 when he took command of *Kagohl* 3.

His primary assignment was the bombing of London and it was to this end that he initially made himself unpopular with the German

*A Gotha bomber squadron preparing for a raid on England.*

High Command. Kleine maintained that the bombing of London would serve no real purpose and would in fact hinder a possible peace plan. However he set about planning his first raid, but decided against London. Instead, he targeted the port of Harwich and the Royal Naval Air Station at Felixstowe. On 4 July 1917, 25 Gotha bombers took off toward the Belgian coast. By the time they reached the sea, seven of the bombers had turned back with engine problems

*Kapitänleutnant Rudolf Kleine; Oberleutnant Gerlich and Manfred von Richthofen in deep discussion outside a hangar at Gontrode in 1917.*

whilst the remainder headed north toward the Suffolk coast where the group split into two flights. On reaching Harwich one flight unloaded its deadly cargo, but fortunately for the inhabitants only two of the bombs actually dropped on the town, the remainder falling into the sea. The other flight attacked Felixstowe, this time with more success. A number of bombs fell on the naval air station, destroying one aircraft and severely damaging several others. The casualties were not excessively high, but 17 died and 29 were wounded. All the German aircraft returned safely, despite 83 Allied aircraft being scrambled from airfields in Kent and Essex with not even one making contact.

During the next couple of months Kleine planned and carried out six bombing missions on London, and on 4 October 1917 he was awarded Germany's highest award, the *Pour le Mérite*. Then on 12 December, during an attack on Ypres, his flight came under attack from Allied fighter aircraft. Kleine's plane was raked from nose to tail, killing both him and his crew, and crashed in no man's land, the bodies being recovered later by German troops.

### Hauptmann Hermann KÖHL

(1888–1938)

The son of a Bavarian general, Hermann Köhl was born in Neu-Ulm, Bavaria, on 15 April 1888. It was only natural that he should follow in his father's footsteps, and on leaving school he joined the Army as a cadet. On graduating he was commissioned as a Leutnant in Bavarian Infantry Regiment Nr. 20, and at the outbreak of war in 1914 was posted to the Western Front. In October 1915 Köhl was badly wounded in intense fighting which resulted in his hospitalisation. On returning to his unit in January 1915 he was awarded the Iron Cross 2nd Class. Köhl then applied for transfer to the newly formed German Army Air Service, much to the annoyance of his father who was not convinced that aeroplanes were for soldiers. Köhl was accepted and posted to flying school where in the spring of 1915 he was awarded his pilot's badge.

For the first few months of his new career Köhl was a reconnaissance pilot and flew a number of missions in support of the artillery and infantry. Then in October 1915 he was transferred to a newly formed *Bombengeschwader*. The squadron trained together, perfecting their bombing techniques, until February 1916 when they started their bombing raids. The initial raids were not great successes, but on the nights of 6 and 7 November 1916 Köhl and his crew attacked the French ammunition depot at Ceresy. The resulting explosion could be seen and heard for miles and the attack caused the French serious munition problems, albeit for only a short period. The success of this raid earned Köhl the command of *Bombengeschwader* (*Bogohl*) 7.

The *Bogohl* was equipped with the Gotha C type bomber and Köhl concentrated on railway stations and ammunition dumps. He gained considerable success when he attacked two of the French Army's largest ammunition dumps with devastating effect. After the second attack, Köhl was awarded the *Pour le Mérite*. He was one of only two *Bombengeschwader* commanders to be given this honour, the other being Ernst Brandenburg. The award, given for over 800 operations, came just after one of the squadron's most dangerous missions, a low-level attack on the largest ammunition depot of the French. On the night of 20/21 May 1918 the squadron of Gothas flew at under 200 feet to the French ammunition depot near Blargies, south-west of Amiens. The raid was a complete success, but it was too late for the German Army.

On another raid in July 1918 the squadron came up against some of the strongest opposition in the air that they had ever encountered, and during the attempt to move away from the target Köhl's bomber was forced down behind enemy lines. Together with his co-pilot and observer-gunner, they set fire to the aircraft and attempted to reach their own lines, but the three crew members were captured and sent to a POW camp. In September Köhl managed to escape and made his way back to Germany however, by this time the war was nearly over and Köhl left the Army, although not aviation. He joined the Junkers company and helped create new civil air routes in Europe and within Germany. But his sense of adventure was not dead. On 13 April 1928, after a 36½-hour flight, his Junkers W.33 'Bremen' landed on Greenly Island, Labrador, after flying across the

*Portrait shot of Hauptmann Hermann Köhl wearing his Pour le Mérite.*

*French ammunition dumps
exploding after being bombed
by Bombengeschwader 7.*

Atlantic. Köhl was accompanied on the flight by another German, Baron von Hünfeld and an Irishman, Commander J Fitzmaurice. The three intrepid aviators were fêted in New York and Washington, putting German aviation firmly back on the map. Hermann Köhl died ten years later on 7 October 1938.

## Leutnant Otto KÖNNECKE
(1892–1956)

Born in Strasbourg on 20 September 1892, the son of a carpenter, Otto Könnecke seemed destined to follow in his father's footsteps after qualifying from the Building Trade School at Frankfurt-am-Main in 1909. He was a carpenter's assistant for two years, then in 1911, bored with his mundane life, he volunteered for military service with Railroad Regiment Nr.3 at Hanau. After two years he was transferred to FEA 4 at Metz and promoted to Unteroffizier. It was at Metz that Könnecke learned to fly and when war was declared the following year he was already a qualified NCO flying instructor. Although there was a desperate need for pilots at the beginning of the war, there was an even greater need for instructors and he was to stay at Metz as an instructor until 3 December 1916. The Germans at this point in the war had lost a large number of pilots in France, so pilots from Macedonia were sent to the Western Front and new and less experienced fighter pilots were sent to replace them. Otto Könnecke was one of the inexperienced pilots, battlewise, who were posted to join *Jasta* 25.

On 9 January Könnecke claimed his first 'kill', but it was unconfirmed. The following month he opened his tally on 5 February when, whilst on patrol over north-west Moglia, he shot down a Henri Farman from Serbian Air Park No.30. The following day he increased his tally by shooting down another Farman from the Serbian *Escadrille* F.98. Then he, like the pilots before him, was posted back to the Western Front to join AFP 2 in March 1917 as a reconnaissance pilot, and in April he joined *Jasta* 5. It was there that he joined up with two other NCO pilots, Fritz Rumey and Joseph Mai, the three later becoming known as the 'Golden Triumvirate' and between them scoring 109 victories by the end of the war. By the end of 1917 Otto Könnecke, in his distinctive Albatros D.V, with its green fuselage, the tail edged in red and a black and white chequerboard marker edged in red just ahead of the black cross on the fuselage, had raised his tally to 11.

*Portrait of Leutnant Otto Könnecke in leather flying clothing.*

Könnecke continued to score steadily and his tally rose until on 12 May his skill and dedication were recognised by the High Command and he was awarded the Golden Military Merit Cross. The following month, on 15 June, he was commissioned in the rank of Leutnant and this was followed on 20 July, when his tally stood at 23, with the award of the Knight's Cross with Swords of the Hohenzollern House Order. One month later he had raised his tally to 32 and with it came Germany's highest honour, the *Pour le Mérite*, making him one of only five airmen to be awarded both the *Pour le Mérite* <u>and</u> the Golden Military Merit Cross.

Otto Könnecke finished the war with a total of 35 victories. In 1926 he joined the newly formed Lufthansa as a pilot, then in 1935, with the birth of the Luftwaffe, he enlisted and became Commandant of the flying schools with the rank of Major. He died in Germany on 25 January 1956.

## Oberleutnant Heinrich Claudius KROLL
(1894–1930)

*Portrait of Leutnant Heinrich Claudius Kroll wearing his Pour le Mérite, Iron Cross 1st Class and his pilot's badge. The troddel at the bottom of the picture is from his sabre.*

The son of a schoolmaster, Heinrich Kroll was born on 3 November 1894 at Flatsby, Flensburg, near Kiel. Kroll seemed destined to follow in his father's footsteps and was studying to become a schoolmaster when the First World War broke out. He immediately volunteered to join the Army and serve with Fusilier Regiment Nr.86, but was sent to join Reserve Infantry Regiment Nr.92 at the front, where with only the barest of training he was soon in the thick of the action. He proved to be an extremely able soldier and within a year had been awarded the Iron Cross 2nd Class and granted a commission as Leutnant.

Kroll had been watching the birth of the German Army Air Service with great interest, and late in 1915 applied for a transfer. After a number of requests he was finally accepted, and in January 1916 was sent to flying training school. After graduating at the end of April, Kroll was posted to FA 17 as a reconnaissance pilot flying Rumpler two-seaters. At his own request he asked to be trained as a fighter pilot and was sent to *Jastaschule*. On completion of his training he was posted to *Jasta* 9 at the beginning of November 1916.

His initial encounter with the enemy was not a memorable one and during his first mission on 24 November his aircraft was shot up and he was forced to land. He was unharmed although his pride was somewhat dented. However, he continued to fly patrols and on 12 February 1917 was awarded the Iron Cross 1st Class. On 1 May 1917 he opened his tally by shooting down a Spad whilst on patrol in his Albatros over west Moronvillers. By the end of the month he had increased his tally to five

*Rumpler C.1 approaching its airfield after a reconnaissance patrol.*

confirmed and one unconfirmed. The fifth victory was particularly pleasing to him as it was the French ace, René Dorme, who had 23 German pilots and their aircraft to his credit.

Kroll was given command of *Jasta* 24 on 1 July and celebrated it by claiming his sixth victim, an SE5 of 56 Squadron, RFC, on 20 July. Seven days later he was shot down in flames during a battle over Menin, but miraculously he was able to land the flaming Albatros D.V and walk away unhurt. Kroll continued to score victories steadily and by the end of the year had raised his tally to 15. The new year started well for Heinrich Kroll as he scored four more victories in the January, raising his tally to 19, and after his 20th victory he was awarded the Knight's Cross of the Hohenzollern House Order on 22 February 1918. The following month he was awarded Germany's highest honour, the *Pour le Mérite* and promotion to Oberleutnant. Another award on 18 June, the Knight's Cross 2nd Class with Swords of the Order of Albert, brought more recognition. On 27 July Kroll had a further lucky escape when he was again shot down with his aircraft in flames and once more walked away unhurt. But his luck changed on 14 August when he was attacked whilst on patrol and was badly injured in his shoulder. The injury was so bad that it effectively ended his combat career and he was obliged to sit out the rest of the war.

In 1928 he joined the Hamburg Flying Club after successfully operating a business. One year later he closed the business down and became a commercial pilot, returning to the world he knew best. Heinrich Kroll died in Hamburg on 21 February 1930 of pneumonia.

### Leutnant der Reserve Arthur LAUMANN
(1894–1970)

Arthur Laumann was born in Essen on 4 July 1894. Like most of his contemporaries Laumann had an uneventful childhood and it was the outbreak of the First World War that would change his life for ever. When the war started he volunteered and joined Field Artillery Regiment Nr.83. For the next two years Laumann fought on the Western and Eastern Fronts, and was awarded the Iron Cross 2nd Class and was given a commission as Leutnant. Over the space of a year he wrote numerous requests for transfer to the German Army Air Service and in August 1917 they acceded to his request.

Laumann was sent for training and on graduating was presented with his certificate and pilot's badge and posted to FA(A) 265 as a reconnaissance pilot. It is interesting to note that FA(A) 265 was commanded by his brother. In the May, Laumann was posted to *Jasta* 66 as a fighter pilot although he had not been given any training; however, it soon became apparent that he was a natural fighter pilot and he opened his account by shooting down a Spad 2 whilst over Couvrelles. It was a happy day for Laumann but a sad one for the *Jasta* as its commander, Rudolph Windisch, was shot down and killed. In the following two months Arthur Laumann had raised his tally to 15 and taken command of *Jasta* 66.

On 14 August 1918 Laumann was posted to *Jasta* 10, in JG 1 to replace another of Germany's top aces, Erich Löwenhardt, who had

*Portrait of Leutnant Arthur Laumann seated in the cockpit of his Fokker D.VII preparing for take-off.*

been killed. His Fokker D.VII was distinctive as it had a mono-grammed 'AL' on the side of the fuselage. Laumann was rewarded on 29 September 1918 with the award of the Iron Cross 1st Class and the Knight's Cross of the Hohenzollern House Order. His tally had been raised to 28 at this point and was recognised by the High Command who awarded him the *Pour le Mérite*. Arthur Laumann stayed as commander of *Jasta* 10 until the end of the war.

During the period between the wars Laumann worked as an instructor but joined the newly formed Luftwaffe in 1935 and became the commander of the new JG Richthofen squadron. He survived the Second World War and became the German Air Attaché to Yugoslavia and Greece. He died of a stroke in Münster on 18 November 1970.

## Leutnant der Reserve Gustav LEFFERS
(1892–1916)

The son of a naval officer, Gustav Leffers was born on 2 January 1892 in Wilhelmshaven. His interest lay in all things mechanical and he was studying naval engineering just prior to the start of the First World War. At the outbreak of war Leffers immediately volunteered for the Aviation Service; he was accepted and sent for flying training to FEA 2 at Aldershof during the autumn and winter of 1914. Leffers graduated in February 1915 and was posted on 14 February to FFA 32 as a pilot flying LVG.Bs, initially on reconnaissance missions.

On 21 March 1915 Gustav Leffers was promoted to Unteroffizier, to Vizefeldwebel the following month, and on 29 May to Offiziersstellvertreter. His race up the promotion ladder came to a halt on 25 July when he was given a commission as Leutnant. Leffers was then given training as a fighter pilot, graduating on 15 September, and he was assigned to FA 32's fighter unit *Kek* 'B' (Bertincourt). The first Fokker Eindecker arrived on 5 November and Leffers was asked to test it. He crashed it on landing, and although the aircraft was destroyed he walked away unhurt – not quite the start he would have wished for with his new unit.

Gustav Leffers opened his tally on 5 December 1915 when, whilst on patrol over Achiet-le-Grand, he shot down a BE2c of 13 Squadron, RFC, and on 29 December another BE2c of 8 Squadron, RFC. By the end of March 1916 his tally had risen to four and he had been awarded the Iron Cross 1st and 2nd Class. His unit *Kek* 'B' was moved

*Portrait of Leutnant Gustav Leffers wearing his* Pour le Mérite, Iron Cross 2nd Class, Knight's Cross with Swords of the Hohenzollern House Order and Oldenburg Friedrich August Cross. *Below these medals can be seen the Iron Cross 1st Class and his pilot's badge.*

*Gustav Leffers in the peaked cap and two fellow pilots leaning against a Halberstadt D.Scout.*

to become *Abwehr Kommando Nord* (AKN) on 31 May 1916, reverting back to *Kek* 'B' at the end of July when it became officially known as *Jasta* 1. Leffers was awarded the Knight's Cross of the Hohenzollern House Order and two classes of the Oldenburg Friedrich August Cross at the end of June 1916.

An FE2b on 9 July 1916, a Martinsyde G 100 on 31 August, and three more Allied aircraft by the beginning of November, brought his tally to nine and earned Leffers the award of the *Pour le Mérite*. Then on 27 December 1916, whilst on patrol over Cherisy, near Wancourt, he clashed with FE2s from 11 Squadron, RFC, and after a long fight was shot down and killed. He was buried with full military honours at Wilhelmshaven on 4 January 1917. Gustav Leffers was 24 years old.

## Oberst Hermann von der LEITH-THOMSEN
(1867–1942)

Born in Flensburg, Prussia, on 10 March 1867, Hermann von der Leith-Thomsen was the son of a wealthy farmer. His early years were taken up with schooling and then helping his father on the farm. At the age of 16 he joined the Army as a cadet and upon graduating in 1889 he was posted to Pioneer Battalion Nr.9 as a Leutnant. Over the next few years his organisational skills were honed to such an extent that he was sent to the Prussian War Academy in 1909. After graduating Leith-Thomsen was given the position of Chief of the Technical Section of the German Greater General Staff, a position he held until the outbreak of the First World War.

*Oberst Hermann von der Leith-Thomsen sitting at his desk.*

In May 1914 he was promoted to Oberleutnant and assigned as General Staff Officer with the Inspection of the Air and Ground Transportation System. However, Leith-Thomsen was not a desk soldier and on 26 August 1914 he took part in the Battle of Tannenberg, during which General Ludendorff's army totally annihilated the Russian Army. Leith-Thomsen distinguished himself to the extent that he was awarded the Iron Cross 2nd Class and one month later was assigned to the General Command of the Reserve Corps 24 as a staff officer. Whilst with Reserve Corps 24 he took part in the Battle of Ypres and in the winter campaigns in the Carpathian Mountains.

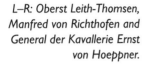

*L–R: Oberst Leith-Thomsen, Manfred von Richthofen and General der Kavallerie Ernst von Hoeppner.*

The newly formed German Army Air Service was beginning to make its presence felt around this time, but it was still raw and needed the steady hand of someone with good organisational skills and the ability to cut red tape. Oberleutnant Hermann von der Leith-Thomsen was just the man. At the beginning of 1915 he was appointed Chief of Field Flying Systems with the German Army Air Service, responsible only to the Commanding General of the Air Strike Forces. One year later he was appointed Chief of the General Staff to the Commanding General of the Air Strike Forces.

Prior to Leith-Thomsen being able to put his organisational skills to work on the German Army Air Service, it had only about 100 pilots and 150 aircraft, but in the two years under his guidance the number of pilots grew to over 5,000. General Erich Ludendorff paid tribute to him by saying, 'It is due to Major Leith-Thomsen's strong creative powers that Germany should be grateful for developing its Air Strike Forces so successfully.' On 8 April 1917 Hermann von der Leith-Thomsen was awarded Germany's highest honour, the *Pour le Mérite* and promoted to Oberst. At the end of the war, he took part in the de-activation of the German Army Air Service under the Treaty of Versailles, and for a short period was Head of the War Ministry Aviation Department.

In 1935, with the war clouds once more looming on the horizon, Leith-Thomsen again offered his services and was given the rank of Generalmajor by Adolf Hitler personally. He was assigned to the Luftwaffe section of the War Department and immediately put his organisational skills to work. Two years later he was promoted to Generalleutnant and in 1939 to General der Flieger. Generalleutnant Hermann von der Leith-Thomsen died of a heart attack on 5 August 1942 at the age of 75.

## Hauptmann Leo LEONHARDY
(1880–1928)

Leo Leonhardy was born on 13 November 1880 in the small town of Rastenburg, East Prussia. After leaving school in 1895 he joined the Army as a cadet and upon graduating in 1900 as a Leutnant he joined the East Prussian Infantry. Just prior to the outbreak of war Leonhardy applied for a transfer to the newly formed German Army Air Service, was accepted in the autumn of 1913 and posted to the Flying School at Johannisthal for training as a pilot.

Ten days after starting his flying training he collided in mid-air with another pupil, and although he managed to land the aircraft, the resulting crash left him with the most horrendous injuries. He suffered a skull fracture, a broken breastbone, a broken nose, two breaks in his spine, broken legs and various other injuries, and was rushed to hospital at Wiesbaden where, after numerous operations, they managed basically to rebuild him. After over a year in hospital he was declared fit for active duty and posted to the Inspectorate of Flying in Berlin. Using his considerable manipulative skills he managed to persuade the High Command that he was fit enough to return to active duty in the field and in the summer of 1915 Leonhardy was posted to the Army Airfield of the Southern Army in Muncacz. Within weeks he was flying again, albeit secretly at first. Then after three months he applied for flying duties as an observer

*Portrait shot of Hauptmann Leo Leonhardy wearing his Pour le Mérite, Iron Cross 2nd Class, Knight's Cross with Swords of the Hohenzollern House Order and the 2nd Class Cross of the Princely Hohenzollern House Order.*

and was posted to Field Flying Unit 59 together with his friend and confidant, Leutnant Kohlhepp, who had secretly worked with him during the previous months.

Leonhardy and his pilot flew numerous artillery and infantry reconnaissance missions during 1916 for which he was promoted to Oberleutnant and awarded the Iron Cross 2nd Class. Then, in September 1916, Leonhardy was posted back to Flying Training School at Johannisthal for training as a pilot and on graduating in January 1917 he was posted to FA 25, a bomber squadron. After flying a number of missions Leonhardy took command of *Bombengeschwader* VI in the summer of 1917. He was promoted to Hauptmann and awarded the Knight's Cross of the Hohenzollern House Order. Leonhardy led a number of missions against the Allies, but one, on 18 February 1918, was to be a memorable one for him and his crew.

The attack was on the Allied airfield at Malzieu-ville, where his squadron dropped over 300 bombs, destroying 10 hangars and 13 Nieuport fighters, together with a fuel and ammunition dump that supplied the field. This was to be the main thrust of his squadron and during the next three months he raided a number of small airfields. In May 1918 the squadron, led by Leonhardy, carried out a raid on the French bomb and fuel dump at Étaples causing considerable damage, for which he received the Iron Cross 1st Class. On 2nd October, after completing over 83 missions, Hauptmann Leo Leonhardy was awarded the *Pour le Mérite*.

When the war ended Leonhardy became an observer again, but this time it was to watch the destruction of German aircraft in accordance with the Versailles Treaty. He retired from military service in 1919 suffering from ill health, and died in Berlin on 12 July 1928.

### Hauptmann Bruno LOERZER
(1891–1960)

Bruno Loerzer was born in Berlin on 22 January 1891. At the age of 17 he became a cadet with the *Badisches Infanterie Regiment Prinz Wilhelm* Nr.112. Later he was accepted at military school and after graduating rejoined his old regiment in January 1913, by now with the rank of Leutnant. It was in this regiment that Leutnant Bruno Loerzer met Hermann Göring and the two of them were to become inseparable throughout their military careers. However, Bruno

Loerzer soon tired of the infantry and applied for flying school, for which he was accepted. In August 1914 he started flying training and on graduating in the October was sent to FA 25 as a reconnaissance pilot. In the meantime his close friend Hermann Göring was having problems with the authorities back at the regiment and was on the point of being court-martialled, when in October Göring decided to join his friend Loerzer as his observer. It appears that the regiment was glad to see the back of him and approved his transfer unofficially, but it was only out of respect for Göring's father, the former Governor of German South-West Africa and his influential friends, that they did not pursue the matter. For the next seven months Loerzer and Göring flew mission after mission and were awarded the Iron Cross 2nd Class on 7 March 1915. But by the end of June 1915, Bruno Loerzer was getting tired of just carrying out observation flights, asked to be transferred to a fighter squadron and was duly transferred to FA 60 then to FA(A) 203.

On completion of his fighter training he was posted to *Kek* Jametz, where, on 21 March 1916, he recorded his first victory. Ten days later he had raised his tally to two and was posted on to *Jasta* 5 late in 1916, then to *Jasta* 17. On 18 January 1917 he was given command of *Jasta* 26. By the end of 1917 his personal tally had risen to 20. Honours were bestowed upon him before the year was out: the Knight's Cross with Swords of the Hohenzollern House Order and the Iron Cross 1st Class. Finally on 12 March he was awarded the *Pour le Mérite* and nine days later he was given command of *Jagdgeschwader* Nr.III. With that command came the Fokker D.V IIs powered by a BMW engine and this aircraft was to inflict heavy casualties on Allied fighters right up to the end of the war.

*Portrait of Bruno Loerzer wearing his* Pour le Mérite *and the medal ribbons of the* Iron Cross 2nd Class and Knight's Cross with Swords of the Hohenzollern House Order.

Bruno Loerzer still continued to fly, usually with *Jasta* 26 alongside his younger brother, who before the war had been a pastor. In the October of 1918 he was promoted to Hauptmann and by the end of the war had raised his tally of victories to 44. During the Second World War he rose rapidly through the ranks to Generalleutnant of

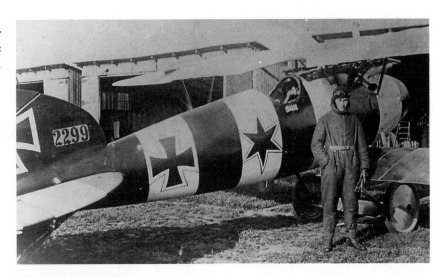

*Hauptmann Bruno Loerzer standing beside his Albatros D.V at Jagdgeschwader Nr.3.*

the Luftwaffe, and was awarded the Iron Cross 1st Class and later the Knight's Cross of the Iron Cross. When he was promoted to Generaloberst it was quite obvious to all that his long-term friendship with Field Marshal Hermann Göring had a great influence on the decision. Bruno Loerzer died on 23 August 1960.

## Oberleutnant Erich LÖWENHARDT

(1897–1918)

*Portrait of Erich Löwenhardt as Leutnant wearing his Pour le Mérite.*

The son of a doctor, Erich Löwenhardt was born in Breslau on 7 April 1897. His education was at a military cadet school in Lichterfelde and at the outset of war he was posted to Infantry Regiment Nr.141. His regiment was moved almost immediately to the Eastern Front where, on 2 October 1914, he was commissioned in the rank of Leutnant. At the end of October he was wounded quite badly and was awarded the Iron Cross 2nd Class. On returning to his unit at the beginning of January 1915 after being discharged from hospital, he was assigned to duties in the Carpathian Mountains. It was whilst in action there that he saved the lives of five wounded soldiers. For this heroic feat he was awarded the Iron Cross 1st Class, and transferred to the Alpine Corps. In October 1915 he requested a transfer to the German Army Air Service as an observer and this was granted. After training, and nearly a year as an observer, Löwenhardt requested pilot training and was posted to FA(A) 265 early in 1916. After a year as a reconnaissance pilot he undertook fighter training early in 1917 and upon graduation was posted to *Jasta* 10 in March 1917.

A week after arriving at *Jasta* 10 Löwenhardt scored his first victory when he destroyed a French observation balloon belonging to 58 *Cie* over Recicourt. By September he had raised his tally to five and almost got himself killed when he was wounded in a dogfight with a British fighter, managing to force-land his aircraft near Roulers. Then on 6 November, with his tally raised to eight, his lower wing broke whilst in combat and again he had to make a forced landing near Winkel St Eloi.

The new year started well for Löwenhardt when, on 5 January, he destroyed another observation balloon, bringing the number of balloons he had brought down to five. Another two balloons followed on 12 and 15 January, together with a BF2b on 18 January. By the end of March he had raised his tally to 15. One week short of his 21st birthday he was appointed commander of *Jasta* 10, one of the youngest commanders in the German Army Air Service. On 11 May, with his tally at 20, he was awarded the Knight's Cross with Swords of the Hohenzollern House Order. Then on 31 May Erich Löwenhardt was awarded

*Leutnant Erich Löwenhardt standing in front of his Fokker Triplane.*

Germany's most prestigious honour, the *Pour le Mérite*. Löwenhardt continued his relentless destruction of Allied aircraft and by the end of July 1918 his tally had risen to 47. During the months of June and July he had been acting commander of the *Jagdgeschwader*, an incredible responsibility for a man who was still only 21.

On 8 August 1918 a patrol led by Löwenhardt encountered a patrol of Sopwith Camels. Löwenhardt himself accounted for three whilst the rest scattered, which brought his tally to 50, the second of only three German pilots to reach this figure. Then tragedy struck on 10 August whilst engaged in a dogfight with a SE5a from 56 Squadron, RAF. Löwenhardt had just shot down an SE5a when he collided in mid-air with Leutnant Alfred Wenz, a member of *Jasta* 11 whose patrol had joined up with that of *Jasta* 10. Both pilots took to their parachutes but Löwenhardt's failed to open and he was killed.

## Hauptmann Karl MENCKHOFF

(1883-1948)

Born on 4 April 1883 at Herford, Westphalia, Karl Menckhoff joined the German Army at the age of 20 in 1903. His time in the Army was short-lived for within six weeks he was taken ill with acute appendicitis and invalided out. He returned to Herford where he stayed for the next 11 years until war broke out in 1914 when he immediately volunteered and joined Infantry Regiment No.106 at Leipzig. Such was the demand for men at the time that his training was a matter of collecting his uniform, cleaning his rifle and heading for the Front Line at Alsace-Lorraine and ultimately the Battle of the Marne. Menckhoff was an aggressive soldier and rapidly made his mark. Towards the end of his first year as a soldier he was selected for a mission behind the lines, dressed in French uniform, for which he was awarded the Iron Cross 1st Class, but within months he was seriously wounded and returned to Herford to recuperate.

*Portrait of Hauptmann Karl Menckhoff when a Leutnant wearing his* Pour le Mérite *and the ribbon of the Iron Cross 2nd Class and the Knight's Cross with Swords of the Hohenzollern House Order.*

Unser erfolgreicher Kampfflieger

His recovery was extremely slow and when he finally completed his convalescence he was deemed to be unfit for infantry duties. So Karl Menckhoff immediately applied for flying duties and was accepted. During his training it was discovered that his aggression on the ground was matched only by his aggression in the air. He took to flying naturally and was a good pilot, but on the ground his maverick and cavalier attitude toward army discipline and etiquette caused problems. He may have been a good fighter, but he was not a good soldier and it was only the fact that his instructors maintained that his exceptional flying ability outweighed his indifference toward the rule book that kept him in the German Army Air Service. The fact that Germany was in desperate need of pilots may also have had something to do with it.

His first posting was to the Eastern Front where he gained a great deal of flying knowledge but very little combat experience. Early in 1916 he was recalled for duty as an instructor, but his aggressive nature soon made it clear that he would be far better employed with a fighting squadron, so he was posted to Flamars for a special short course in air combat, and in early 1917 to *Jasta* 3 in Flanders with promotion to Vizefeldwebel. Within days he had scored his first victory, a Nieuport XXIII of 29 Squadron, RFC. Two more had followed by the end of the month and by September he had raised his tally to 12, although on 28 September he was himself shot down and wounded by aircraft from 56 Squadron, RFC. After recovering from his wounds he returned to *Jasta* 3, threw himself back into the war and by the end of 1917 had raised his tally to 18. In February 1918 he was given a commission and command of *Jasta* 72. He was also awarded the Knight's Cross with Swords of the Hohenzollern House Order which was followed on 23 April 1918 by the award of the *Pour le Mérite*.

The following four months saw Karl Menckhoff's tally rise to 39, then three days after his 40th victory he met his equal when he encountered Lt William Avery of the 95th Aero Squadron, USAS. After a short fight Menckhoff was forced down behind Allied lines and taken prisoner. Following interrogation he was transferred to Camp Montoire near Orléans where he joined an ever-growing number of pilots from the German Army Air Service. His impatience was fuelled by his aggression and tired of waiting for repatriation he escaped on 23 August and headed for Switzerland. One week later he crossed the border, remaining there until the end of the war. Seeing the state of Germany after the war, Karl Menckhoff decided to stay in Switzerland and set up in business, remaining there until his death in 1948.

## Leutnant Max Ritter von MÜLLER
(1887–1918)

Born on 1 January 1887 in Rottenburg, Lower Bavaria, Max Müller rose from relative obscurity to become one of Germany's top fighter aces of the First World War. After serving an apprenticeship as a locksmith, Müller joined the Army in 1912 as a driver and it was discovered that he had a natural mechanical aptitude. He soon came to the notice of his superiors and was assigned as chauffeur to the Bavarian War Minister. By this time Müller had acquired an interest in aviation and it is said that every time he opened the door for the minister he asked to be transferred to the German Army Air Service. His persistence was rewarded, probably more out of a desire to be rid of him, than a wish to help him.

*Leutnant Max Müller standing in front of his Albatros D.V.*

He was posted to the army flying school at Schliessheim on 1 December 1913. After four months of training he qualified as a pilot and received his certificate and Bavarian Pilot's Badge on 4 April 1914. With the situation worsening by the day, the German Army was mobilised and this included the air service. Müller was posted to FA

1b as a reconnaissance pilot and carried out several missions. On 18 August he was just taking off when his engine failed and the aircraft plunged to the ground breaking both Müller's legs in the impact. On his recovery he was back in the air, this time with the rank of Offiziersstellvertreter. Then, for flying an extremely dangerous photographic mission on 13 December 1915, he was awarded the Bavarian Bravery Medal in Silver. By May the following year he had made over 160 missions as a reconnaissance pilot and had been awarded the Iron Cross 1st and 2nd Class and the Bavarian Military Merit Cross 3rd Class with Crown and Swords. By now he was one of the most experienced reconnaissance pilots in the German Army Air Service, but he wanted more, so he applied for transfer to a fighter squadron. He was transferred reluctantly to single-seater training at Mannheim where, on 18 May 1916, after graduating, he was posted to *Kek* 'B' which was attached to FA 32.

Müller remained at *Kek* 'B' until 1 September 1916 when he was posted to *Jasta* 2. His experience soon helped him settle into the squadron, and on 10 October he scored his first victory when he shot down a DH.2 of 24 Squadron, RFC. By the end of the year his tally had risen to five. The formation of a new *Jasta*, 28, prompted the move of a number of experienced pilots, including Max Müller and Leutnant Ray, to form the backbone of the squadron. By the end of May Müller's tally had risen to 13 making him the top-scoring fighter pilot in the *Jasta*. On 26 August the unprecedented step was taken to promote him to Leutnant in the Regular Army, for usually these promotions were in the Reserve and this was the first time this had ever occurred.

Müller grew from strength to strength and by the end of September 1917 had raised his tally to 27 and with it had earned the *Pour le Mérite*, making him the most decorated pilot next to Manfred von Richthofen in the German Army Air Service. A well-earned leave resulted in him asking to rejoin his old squadron, *Jasta* 2, also known as *Jasta* Boelcke, to assist his old friend Erwin Böhme in bringing it into shape. His request was granted and he was posted to *Jasta* 2 on 3 November 1917. On 6 January 1918, following the death of the commanding officer Leutnant Walter von Bülow, and with his own tally standing at 36, he took over command of *Jasta* 2. Three days later whilst on patrol over Moorslede, he and his patrol attacked an RE.8 of 21 Squadron, RFC. As he did so, two SE5as, flown by very experienced fighter pilots, Captains F O Soden and R L Childlaw-Roberts, jumped him at the same time from above and behind. Müller's aircraft reeled from the assault and, spiralling towards the ground, burst into flames. As the flames reached the cockpit, Müller, who was not wearing a parachute, jumped to his death rather than burn.

After the war Müller was posthumously awarded the Knight's Cross of the Military Max Joseph Order which conferred a knighthood on him, backdated to 11 November 1917. Leutnant Max Ritter von Müller was 31 years old.

### Oberleutnant Albert MÜLLER-KAHLE
(1894–?)

The future holder of Germany's highest decoration – the *Pour le Mérite* – was born on 29 June 1894, the son of a Lutheran pastor. When the First World War began he enlisted as a cadet in the 20th Foot Artillery Regiment, but after a year he requested a transfer to the German Army Air Service. He was accepted and in the January of 1916 underwent training as an artillery spotter and observer. Müller-Kahle graduated in the spring of 1916 and was posted to *Flieger Abteilung* 202, later serving with FAs 215, 47 and 6, and seeing active service on the Western Front in sectors Douai, the Somme and along the North Sea coast.

*Portrait shot of Oberleutnant Albert Max Müller-Kahle wearing his Pour le Mérite. The medal ribbon of the Knight's Cross with Swords of the Hohenzollern House Order can be seen attached to the edge of his 'maternity style' jacket.*

Müller-Kahle became very proficient in calling in artillery fire on specific targets. The Germans began to use heavy artillery mounted on railway tracks and Müller-Kahle was able to direct their fire on important strategic targets such as the coal mines at Béthune. So proficient did Müller-Kahle become in artillery spotting that he was selected early in 1918 to become an observer for the new long-range guns (only eight were made), named the *Kaiser Wilhelm Geschütz*, and designed by Professor Fritz Rausenberger of Krupps, to bombard Paris. These monster guns had originally been designed at the request of the Navy and were manned and controlled by naval personnel, much to the chagrin of the Army. The guns weighed 297 tons, had barrel lengths of 109.25 feet and were mounted on a specially designed railway truck. The barrels of the guns wore out at such a rate that they had to be replaced after 50 shells had been fired.

At 7.15 a.m. on 23 March 1918 one of the *Geschütz* guns, the *Pariskanone*, opened fire on Paris from 110 kilometres behind German lines, with, it is said, Müller-Kahle in the air acting as artillery fire adjuster. Müller-Kahle climbed, apparently to 5,000 metres, then flew to within 39 kilometres of Paris and directed fire. Coming under heavy anti-aircraft fire, and machine-gun fire from British fighters, he managed to complete his spotting and return to base. Over the 20 weeks the weapon was used its shells killed over 1,000 Parisians, including one incident on Good Friday, 29 March, when a shell from the *Pariskanone* crashed through the roof of St Gervais L'Église and exploded in the transept during Mass. Ninety-one worshippers were killed and over a hundred were wounded. This act only made the Germans more hated than ever and before the bombardment of Paris was over even a large number of Germans were against it. For his role as observer, Müller-Kahle was awarded the *Pour le Mérite* on 13 October 1918.

Albert Müller-Kahle survived the war and became a Generalmajor in the Luftwaffe during the Second World War.

*Albert Müller-Kahle as a Generalmajor of the Luftwaffe in the Second World War.*

## Leutnant Max Ritter von MULZER

(1893–1916)

Max Mulzer was born on 9 July 1893 in Kimratshofen, near Kempten, Bavaria, the son of a doctor. He enlisted in the Army as a cadet in 1910 and graduated as an officer cadet on 10 July 1914, joining the 8th Cavalry Regiment. Mulzer was commissioned on 13 December 1914 as a Leutnant after taking part in some of the earliest battles of the war at Peronne, Lille and Épinal, but already his eyes were on the future and in July 1915 he asked to be transferred to the German Army Air Service. Mulzer's request was approved and he was posted to the Army's flying school at Schliessheim on 20 August 1915, where after four months training he graduated, obtaining his flying certificate and Bavarian pilot's badge.

Leutnant Max Mulzer was assigned to FFA 4b on 13 December 1915 and after two months was transferred, along with Oswald Boelcke and Max Immelmann, to FFA 62 where the serious training as a fighter pilot began. On 13 March 1916 he scored his first victory, albeit an unconfirmed one, when he shot down a Morane Saulnier and was awarded the Iron Cross 2nd Class. However he made up for it on 30 March when he shot down a VFB.5 from 11 Squadron, RFC, over north Wancourt. At the beginning of June he was posted to join *Kek* Nord in Russia where he quickly made his presence felt by scoring three more victories in a matter of ten days, bringing his tally to six, for which he was awarded the Iron Cross 1st Class. In June Mulzer

was posted to Douai to join FFA 32, then temporarily with *Kek* 'B', where he increased his tally to eight. The eighth victory brought him the *Pour le Mérite*, making him the first Bavarian to be honoured with Germany's highest award. On 26 September he was further honoured when he received the Knight's Cross of the Military Max Joseph Order. This in effect made him a 'Knight' and allowed his name to be changed from Leutnant Max Mulzer to 'Leutnant Max Ritter von Mulzer'. By the beginning of August, Mulzer had raised his tally to ten.

At the beginning of September 1916 he was assigned to AFP 6 at

Valenciennes to test a number of aircraft. On 26 September 1916 Mulzer took off to test Albatros DI, 4424/16, and during the test flight the aircraft suffered structural failure and crashed, killing him. Leutnant Max Ritter von Mulzer was just 23 years old.

## Leutnant Ulrich NECKEL
(1898–1928)

Ulrich Neckel was born in Bavaria on 23 January 1898, his early childhood being unremarkable like many others of his age at the time. But Neckel was always seeking adventure and at the age of 16, when the First World War began, he volunteered for the Army, and he was sent for training as an artilleryman with the Holstein *Feld Artillerie Regiment* Nr.24. On completing the training in January 1915 he was sent to the Eastern Front and was in action immediately.

*Informal portrait of Leutnant Ulrich Neckel standing in front of his Fokker aircraft.*

Within six months he had been awarded the Iron Cross 2nd Class for distinguishing himself under fire. The terrible conditions and stress of the Eastern Front were beginning to have their effect on Neckel, and he began to think of ways to get out of the cold and the mud. In September 1916 he applied for transfer to the German Army Air Service and was accepted. He was posted to the flying school at Gotha in November 1916 and graduated as a pilot in February 1917.

After joining the Army Air Service in order to get away from the Eastern Front, he was promptly posted back there to join FA 25. After flying a number of reconnaissance missions he applied for training as a fighter pilot, and in the August was sent to *Jastaschule* at Valenciennes. On graduating in the September he was posted to *Jasta* 12 and promoted to Gefreiter. Neckel opened his tally on 21 September 1917 when he shot down a Sopwith Pup from 46 Squadron, RFC, whilst on patrol over east Monchy-le-Preux. By the end of the month he had increased his score to two, after shooting down a DH.5 from 41

Squadron, and his total stood at three by the end of the year.

Such was Ulrich Neckel's success in the first quarter of 1918 that he was commissioned as Leutnant and awarded the Iron Cross 1st Class. By the end of April his tally had risen to ten. Neckel continued to be a thorn in the side of the Allies and had taken his score to 20 by the end of July. At the beginning of September he was transferred to *Jasta* 19 and immediately increased his tally that month to 24. He was awarded the Knight's Cross with Swords of the Hohenzollern House Order on 24 August and was given command of *Jasta* 6 in *Jagdgeschwader* Nr. 1 on 1 September 1917.

His success continued and by the beginning of November 1918 he had increased his score to 26 and had been awarded the coveted *Pour le Mérite*. Ulrich Neckel, together with Carl Degelow, was the last to receive the *Pour le Mérite*, the famous award never being awarded again.

When the Armistice came in November Leutnant Ulrich Neckel's score stood at 30. Not long after the war he contracted tuberculosis and after a very long illness died in Italy on 11 May 1928. He was buried in the Veterans' Cemetery in Berlin.

### Leutnant der Landwehr Friedrich NIELEBOCK
(1882–?)

*Portrait of Leutnant der Landwehr Friedrich Nielebock wearing his* Pour le Mérite.

The son of a retired army officer, Friedrich Nielebock was born in Weissenwarthe, north Germany, on 4 July 1882. An outstanding all-round athlete whilst at school, he later became an expert shot, something that was to hold him in good stead in later years.

When the First World War began in 1914 Nielebock was doing his volunteer reserve duty with the Foot Artillery Regiment at Lauenburg. He realised that his artillery training and experience could be put to best use in the air as an artillery spotter and reconnaissance observer. After a month's observer training Nielebock joined *Flieger Abteilung* 250, remaining with the artillery as an aerial observer for the next four years and becoming well known for the accuracy of his artillery spotting. He was wounded badly on 24

January 1918 during a reconnaissance sortie.

He was awarded the *Pour le Mérite* on 2 June 1918, and his citation – written by his commander Hauptmann Schaffer – is a true record of his service and bravery in combat:

> Since the beginning of the war, with but one month's interruption for Observer training, Leutnant Nielebock was continuously in the Field at Ypres and Wytschaetebogen with ground troops. His eighteen months performance on the Flanders front is uniquely superior. Up to now he has flown 280 sorties. He is an artillery observer and has carried out 196 artillery fire observational sorties, of which 134 were effective. Of 728 newly discovered battery positions, 331 could be attacked at once due to Leutnant Nielebock's wireless messages. He achieved superior results with directed heavy low trajectory fire during night and day. His service in the last attack days deserves special recognition. His artillery, scouting and observation flights, through which he supplied information about the position and activity of the artillery battle, resulted in oral and written praise. During two days of strictly relying on Leutnant Nielebock's reports, the Commanding General of 18 Reserve Corps was able to take measures that were decisive for the success of the subsequent battles. Leutnant Nielebock's work not only deserves recognition in the field of artillery observation, but also in the area of continued progress in artillery flying

*Leutnant Friedrich Nielebock (on the right of the group) with members of* Flieger Abteilung *250 enjoying a relaxed afternoon's socialising.*

activity and in the cooperation of the airmen and the artillery.

Leutnant Friedrich Nielebock survived the war, returned to civilian life to earn professional qualifications in the building trade and became a director of a large company in Venezuela.

### Oberleutnant zur See Theodor OSTERKAMP
(1892–1975)

*Oberleutnant zur See Theodor Osterkamp sitting on the wheel of his Fokker E.V monoplane.*

Born the son of a forestry worker in Düren in the Rhineland on 15 April 1892, Theodor Osterkamp was himself studying forestry when war was declared. Rather than be conscripted into the Army, Osterkamp enlisted in the Naval Flying Corps in August 1914. His initial request was to be trained as a pilot, but the need for observers was greater. On completion of his training, Osterkamp was posted to the Marine Flying Detachment where for the next two years he flew operational missions along the Belgian coast. His success was rewarded with the Iron Cross 2nd Class and his being commissioned in June 1916.

The tedious routine of these missions began to make Osterkamp look toward the single-seat fighter pilots who seemed to have more exciting lives (an error of judgement as he was soon to find out) than he did. In February 1917, Osterkamp applied for fighter-pilot training. In the March he was accepted and graduated on 14 April. He was posted to MFJ I the same week and opened his score on 30 April when he shot down a Sopwith Camel whilst on patrol over Oostkerke. At the end of July 1917 Osterkamp had raised his tally to five and on 20 August was rewarded with the Iron Cross 1st Class and the Knight's Cross of the Hohenzollern House Order. A Spad from *Escadrille* Spa.31 fell to him on 24 September, raising his tally to six. Then in October he was given command of MFJ II and promoted to Oberleutnant.

His first 'baptism under fire' did not exactly

inspire confidence. Whilst on a solo familiari-sation flight in a new Fokker EV monoplane, he was 'jumped' by three Spads, with the end result being that he had to bale out, fortu-nately landing behind his own lines unhurt. At the beginning of 1918 Osterkamp spent time reorganising the unit to make it more efficient and this was reflected in the way that victories started to mount up. By the end of July 1918 Osterkamp's personal tally had risen

*Leutnant zur See Theodor Osterkamp and his observer wrapped in their flying clothes against the cold, standing beside their Rumpler prior to leaving on a reconnaissance mission.*

from 6 to 19 and by the end of August was standing at 23. For this, on 2 September, he received Germany's highest award, the *Pour le Mérite*. The war against the Allies ended in 1918, but he continued to fight in the Baltic area until 1920.

In 1935 Theodor Osterkamp joined the Luftwaffe as it started to rebuild and he was given command of *Jagdfliegerschule* Nr.1 in 1939, a post he held until the following year when he took over command of JG 51. Almost immediately he was in action against the French and in the months of May and July shot down a total of six Allied fighters, which included three Hurricanes and a Spitfire. For this he was awarded the Knight's Cross of the Iron Cross on 22 August 1940. He became Commander of Fighters in northern France and later in Sicily, holding the rank of Generalleutnant. He also became very critical of the High Command and the way they were directing the war in the air, and because of his outspokenness he was retired in 1944. It was probably the tremendous respect that Luftwaffe pilots and ground crews had for him that prevented a worse fate befalling him. Theodor Osterkamp died in Baden-Baden on 2 January 1975 at the age of 83.

## Leutnant Otto PARSCHAU
(1890–1916)

The son of a land-leaser, Otto Parschau was born in Kluznitz, East Prussia, on 11 November 1890. His early childhood was relatively uneventful and on his 20th birthday he joined the 151st Infantry Regiment as a cadet. A year later he received his commission as a Leutnant, but his ambitions were elsewhere. Having watched with great interest the birth of the German Army Air Service he decided he would learn to fly, so he started flight training at Darmstadt at the

*Portrait of Leutnant Otto Parschau wearing his* Pour le Mérite *and the medals of the Iron Cross 2nd Class and Knight's Cross with Swords of the Hohenzollern House Order. The photograph was taken just after Parschau, complete with all his medals and pet dog, had returned from receiving his* Pour le Mérite.

Schlafwagen

Unser Helden-Flieger Leutnant Parschau.

beginning of February 1913, then at Johannisthal and Hannover for further training before graduating on 4 July. His licence number was No.455, which placed him amongst the pioneers of early flying in Germany. Within the first year he had won a number of awards, mostly for long distance flights, including the Honour Prize of Prince Friedrich Sigismund of Prussia at the Ostmark Flight Competition in

1914.

At the outbreak of war Otto Parschau applied to join the German Army Air Service and was accepted immediately. Because of his experience as a long-distance pilot he was immediately posted as a reconnaissance pilot to FA 42 then to FA 261. For his services to reconnaissance work he was awarded the Iron Cross 2nd Class early in 1915. But his experience as a pilot was needed desperately in a fighter squadron and he was transferred to KG 1 flying single-seat Fokkers. He opened his tally on 11 October 1915 when he shot down a Maurice Farman whilst on patrol over Argonne, and had raised his tally to two by the end of the year, notching up a BE2c from 12 Squadron, RFC, whilst over Oostkampe near Bruges.

The early part of 1916 brought another two victories to Parschau, then in the May he was appointed commander of *Kampfgeschwader* No.1 (KG 1) and was awarded the Iron Cross 1st Class and the Knight's Cross with Swords of the Hohenzollern House Order. By the beginning of July he had raised his tally to eight and on 10 July was awarded Germany's highest honour, the *Pour le Mérite*. However, his euphoria was short-lived for on 21 July, whilst on patrol over Grevillers, his squadron was attacked by Allied aircraft, and after a long, fierce battle Otto Parschau was badly wounded in the head and chest. He managed to crash-land his aircraft, but died later from his injuries.

## Oberleutnant Paul Freiherr von PECHMANN
(1889–?)

Paul Pechmann was born on 28 December 1889 at Gaudismühl near Nurenberg. He began his military career by enlisting in the 7th Artillery (Foot) Regiment stationed in Cologne. He was promoted to Leutnant in 1911 and when war broke out he was posted to the *Flieger Abteilung Artillerie* at Wahn. He went with this unit to the front but transferred to *Feldflieger Abteilung* 6. He then saw service as an artillery observer with *Flieger Abteilungs* 215 and 217 on the Flanders section of the Western Front. During his three years service with these units his outstanding abilities brought him several decorations, including the Knight's Cross with Swords of the Hohenzollern House Order.

In the summer of 1917 he was promoted to Oberleutnant and became *Abteilungs Führer* of *Flieger Abteilung (A)* 215. Germany's supreme award, the *Pour le Mérite*, was awarded personally to

*Portrait of Oberleutnant Paul Freiherr von Pechmann wearing his Pour le Mérite and Knight's Cross with Swords of the Hohenzollern House Order. Just below his Iron Cross 1st Class can be seen his observer's badge.*

Pechmann by Kaiser Wilhelm II on 31 July 1917. Included in the citation for the decoration were the words, 'For having carried out over 700 operational sorties against the enemy'. Although he had qualified as a pilot, Pechmann's *Pour Le Mérite* was awarded for services as an observer with *Flieger Abteilungs* 215 and 217. He was the first artillery and reconnaissance flier to gain the *Pour le Mérite*.

In January 1918 Pechmann was given command of *Flieger Abteilung (A)* 217 and played an important reconnaissance role in the German March offensive. One such mission was carried out in fog, and Pechmann flew so low that his aircraft was under almost constant ground fire. When he returned, it was found to have over 150 holes in the wings and fuselage. He flew a number of missions without fighter escort and on one particular one came close to paying the penalty. Pechmann and his pilot were so engrossed with directing artillery fire upon a munitions dump that they failed to see two Sopwith Camels closing on them, and their aircraft was raked with machine-gun fire. With their engine and radiator riddled with bullet holes and with the light fading fast, they managed to glide across the lines to their own side and safety.

Pechmann remained with his unit on the Western Front and was flying during the Battle of Cambrai when the British made use of tanks. He was also responsible for resupplying the hard-pressed German forces with food and ammunition – which he did with distinction.

After the First World War ended Pechmann remained in the German Air Service but retired in 1920 as a Hauptmann.

### Leutnant Fritz PÜTTER
(1895–1918)

Fritz Pütter was born in Dülmen, Westphalia, on 14 January 1895. His childhood was uneventful but an incident on 28 June 1914 was to change not only his life but the lives of millions – the assassination of the Archduke Ferdinand was to send shock waves that were to have catastrophic ramifications worldwide.

War was declared on 4 August 1914 and on 24 August Fritz Pütter joined the Westphalian Infantry Regiment. After scant training he was sent to the Eastern Front and almost immediately was involved in heavy fighting. Early in 1915 Pütter was involved in an incident of heroism that not only earned him the Iron Cross 2nd Class, but a battlefield commission as Leutnant, and on 12 October 1915 he was transferred to the 370th Infantry Regiment. It was then that he started to get interested in the newly formed German Army Air Service and in February 1916 he applied for a transfer, was accepted and posted to FEA 8 at Graudenz on 20 May 1916.

*Portrait of Leutnant Fritz Pütter just after he had received his* Pour le Mérite.

On completion of his flying training, on 9 December 1916, he was posted to FA 251 as a reconnaissance pilot. After two months of flying reconnaissance missions, Pütter requested a transfer to fighter-pilot duties, was sent to *Jastaschule* and on graduating was posted to *Jasta* 9 on 17 March 1917. He opened his tally on 14 April when he shot down a French observation balloon whilst on patrol over east Suippes. By the end of the year he had increased his tally to five, all of which were French observation balloons.

On 12 January 1918 Pütter scored his first victory over another aircraft when he shot down a Spad, but finished the day by adding another balloon to his tally. By the end of January he had added another two aircraft and two balloons, bringing his total to 10. Pütter was awarded the Iron Cross 1st Class in February although the month itself was one of the quietest the *Jasta* had known. He was posted to *Jasta* 68 on 3 February as commandant and spent the month familiarising himself with the aircraft and their pilots. But things were to change in March, and by the end of the month Pütter had shot down another six aircraft bringing his tally to 15. For this he was awarded the Knight's Cross with Swords of the Hohenzollern House Order.

Pütter continued to score steadily against the Allies and by the end of May his tally had risen to 25, and on 31 May he was awarded the *Pour le Mérite*. Tragedy was to strike on 16 July, however, for whilst on patrol he encountered some enemy aircraft and engaged them. During the ensuing dogfight the tracer ammunition in his Fokker caught fire. Although very badly burned he managed to limp back to his base where he was rushed to hospital. Later he was transferred to the burns hospital in Bonn where he died of his injuries on 10 August 1918.

### Oberleutnant Lothar Freiherr von RICHTHOFEN
(1894–1922)

Younger brother of the famous Red Baron – Manfred von Richthofen – Lothar was born on the Richthofen family estate at Breslau on 27 September 1894. Prior to the outbreak of the First World War he joined a cavalry regiment and when war broke out was serving with the 4th Dragoon Regiment. Spurred on by the example of his elder brother he transferred to the German Army Air Service in the autumn of 1915. Serving as an observer with KG 4 he was determined to be a fighter pilot, and after training gained his pilot's certificate in 1916.

On 6 March 1917 he had his first operational posting as a pilot to *Jasta* 11, commanded by his brother Manfred. Flying with *Jasta* 11 he scored his first victory on 28 March 1917 when he shot down FE2b No.7715 of 25 Squadron, RFC. Remarkably, his victory total began to increase almost daily, as on 11 April he shot down two aircraft, another two on 13 April and two more on 14 April 1917. By 30 April he had downed another ten aircraft, taking his tally for April 1917 to 16 confirmed kills and he was awarded the Iron Cross 1st Class to add to his Iron Cross 2nd Class.

*Portrait of Oberleutnant Lothar Freiherr von Richthofen wearing his* Pour le Mérite.

When the first of May dawned Lothar continued his relentless pursuit of Germany's enemies. An FE2d of 25 Squadron fell to his guns, bringing his total to 17 confirmed victories. On 10 May he was awarded the Knight's Cross with Swords of the Hohenzollern House Order, and by 13 May another seven aircraft had been shot down to bring his number of kills to 24. But the 13th proved unlucky for Lothar as he was badly wounded in combat and hospitalised. However, 14 May proved better as, lying in hospital, he was awarded Germany's highest honour for bravery in combat – the *Pour le Mérite*, only five months after the same award had gone to his brother Manfred, the Red Baron.

Lothar returned to flying duty on 24 September 1917 and took command of *Jasta* 11. Six weeks later on 9 November he was back in combat and shot down a BF2b of 8 Squadron near Zonnebeke. On 23 November he added his 26th kill to his score by bringing down another BF2b, but it was to be three months into 1918 before he scored again. On 11 March he shot down a BF2b of 62 Squadron, followed the next day by two more BF2bs.

The next day, 13 March, again proved unlucky for Lothar when he was severely wounded in combat, although it was some consolation that he was promoted to Oberleutnant whilst in hospital, and he was also awarded the Bavarian Military Merit Order 4th Class with Swords. After returning to *Jasta* 11 on 19 July, he shot down his 30th aircraft, a Sopwith Camel of 73 Squadron on 25 July. Ten more enemy aircraft were credited to him during August, three of them in one day, the 8th. His final victories came on 12 August when he brought down two Camels of 98 and 209 Squadrons, making a total of 40 confirmed victories. Again he was badly wounded and did not return to combat, although he survived the war and resumed flying after the Armistice, but died in a flying accident on 4 July 1922.

## Rittmeister Manfred Freiherr von RICHTHOFEN
(1892–1918)

The legendary Red Baron was born at Breslau on 2 May 1892, into the aristocratic Prussian Junker family of Albrecht Freiherr von Richthofen, a Major in the 1st Regiment of Cuirassiers, and the Baroness Kunigunde von Richthofen.

Blue-eyed, blond-haired and of medium height he was destined to leave his mark on aviation history during his short life. At the age of eleven he entered the military school at Wahlstatt, followed by admission to the Royal Prussian Military Academy. Easter 1911 saw him join a famous regiment of lancers, Uhlan Regiment No.1 'Kaiser Alexander III'. In the autumn of 1912 he was commissioned as a Leutnant in the 1st Uhlans. At the outbreak of the First World War he went with his Uhlans into Russian Poland but within two weeks the regiment was transferred to the Meuse in France, where it was allocated to the Crown Prince's 5th German Army.

Trench warfare saw the end of Richthofen's cavalry unit so he was attached to 6th Army Corps and awarded the Iron Cross 2nd Class for active service with the Uhlans, not for infantry service. Not relishing his infantry role he applied for a transfer to the German Army Air Service in May 1915. After four weeks training as an observer at FEA

*Manfred von Richthofen talking with fellow pilots. L–R: unknown; Hauptmann Carganico; Richthofen; von Gerstenberg.*

7 at Cologne and FEA 6 at Grossenheim he was posted to FA 69 on the Eastern Front as an observer in an Albatros B.II. His pilot, Leutnant Zeumer, it was discovered later, was dying from tuberculosis and had a wish to die in action.

In August 1915 Manfred von Richthofen was posted to the 'Mail Carrier Pigeon Unit' at Ostend, the innocuous title being a cover name for a long-range bomber unit training to bomb England. Richthofen had his first taste of aerial combat on 1 September 1915. Flying as observer in an AEG with Leutnant Zeumer he spotted a Royal Flying Corps Farman flying nearby and ordered Zeumer to close to combat. Armed only with a rifle Richthofen opened fire on the Farman but missed with his four shots. The observer in the Farman fired back and scored several hits on Richthofen's AEG. A week later he was flying as observer in an Albatros piloted by Leutnant Osteroth, Zeumer having been admitted to hospital, when he sighted a solitary Farman flying over French lines. Ordering his pilot to attack, Richthofen opened up with his machine-gun and fired 100 rounds at the enemy aircraft. The stricken Farman plunged to earth and crashed behind French lines; however, the victory was unconfirmed and Richthofen was not credited with his first victory.

On 1 October 1915 Richthofen was posted to Metz to join another bomber unit. En route by train he met the already legendary Oswald Boelcke whom he engaged in conversation. Fired by Boelcke's example Richthofen decided to become a pilot and asked Leutnant

Zeumer to teach him to fly. His first attempt to do so ended in disaster when he crashed on landing, but he persisted in his training and on Christmas Day 1915 qualified as a pilot. Posted to Russia, it was not until March 1916 that he returned to the Western Front. Even then he was ordered to fly a two-seater Albatros – not the single-seat fighter he longed for. Undaunted he adapted the two-seater Albatros with a machine-gun on the upper wing that he could fire from the pilot's seat.

On 26 April 1916 he first used his machine-gun in action against a French Nieuport over French Lines. The Nieuport, riddled with bullets, fell from the sky and crashed behind French Lines at Douaumont. Again his victory was unconfirmed. Richthofen had not yet opened his score officially. Eventually he got his dearest wish and joined Oswald Boelcke's *Jasta* on 1 September 1916. He was now in his natural hunter's element flying the new single-seat Albatros D.IIIs of *Jasta* 2. On 17 September Boelcke led his eight-strong *Jasta* into action and sighted eight BE2cs of 12 Squadron, RFC, and six FE2bs of 11 Squadron bombing Marcoing railway station. Richthofen, flying Albatros D.III 491/16, chose an FE2b as his quarry and opened fire but missed the enemy aircraft which retaliated with heavy machine-gun fire. Avoiding the lethal response Richthofen banked out of range then came back under and behind the FE2b. Closing to point blank range, and unseen by the enemy aircraft's crew, he opened a deadly burst of fire on the FE2b's engine and cockpit that wounded both the pilot, Second Lieutenant L B F Morris and his observer, Lieutenant T Rees. The doomed FE2b plunged downwards with the dying pilot Morris managing to land it behind German lines. Richthofen followed it down where he found the pilot mortally wounded and the observer dead.

*Side view of Manfred von Richthofen landing in his all-red Fokker Triplane.*

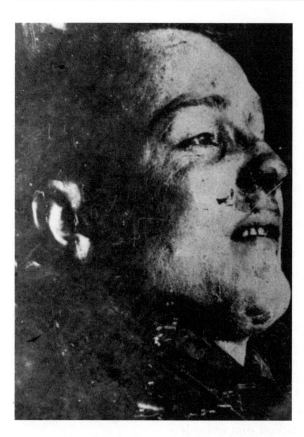

*Close-up of Manfred von Richthofen's face after his body had been recovered from the wreckage of his Fokker Triplane, after being shot down by Australian ground forces.*

Richthofen had scored his first officially confirmed victory, and to mark the event had a silver cup made by a Berlin silversmith. It was to be the first of 80 such cups. By the end of October 1916 Richthofen had six confirmed victories to his credit. His hunter's prowess needed to be demonstrated by his collecting relics from each of his downed adversary's aircraft which were sent to the family home in Silesia for proud display. On 28 October Boelcke was killed in an aerial collision with Erwin Böhme and *Jasta* 2 was renamed *Jasta* Boelcke (Royal Prussian) with Oberleutnant Stephen Kirmaier in command.

Richthofen's victory tally continued to grow and by 20 November 1916 he had ten confirmed kills. Two days later he shot down the Royal Flying Corps's leading ace, Major L G Hawker VC DSO flying a DH2 of 24 Squadron, in an epic aerial dogfight. When Richthofen learned who his opponent had been he flew over British lines and dropped a message to inform 24 Squadron of Major Hawker's death. *Jasta* Boelcke pilots arranged a military funeral for Major Hawker but Richthofen did not attend for it was not the done thing for the victor to attend the funeral of his victim.

Richthofen was promoted to flight commander with *Jasta* Boelcke and had his Albatros aircraft painted bright red to let his aerial opponents know who he was and this led to his most famous title – 'The Red Baron'. When he scored his sixteenth victory on 4 January 1917 the Kaiser awarded him, by special citation, the *Pour le Mérite*. He was only 24 years old and now Germany's national hero.

With the decoration came promotion to Rittmeister (Cavalry Captain) and command of *Jasta* 11. On 11 April 1917 Richthofen had taken his score to 40 confirmed kills and by the end of April it had risen to 52 confirmed. On 30 April he crossed swords with the Canadian ace Billy Bishop (who ended the war with 72 kills) over Drocourt. Try as he might Richthofen could not get the better of Bishop who outflew him and riddled his Albatros with bullets, forcing Richthofen to break off the duel and retreat eastward towards friendly territory.

On 26 June the German High Command grouped *Jastas* into JGs (*Jagdgeschwader* or hunting squadrons) and Richthofen took command of JG 1 that comprised *Jastas* 4, 6, 10 and 11. These JGs were highly mobile and with their aircraft being brightly painted they were soon nicknamed 'Richthofen's Flying Circus'. Richthofen continued to increase his score but when flying his red Albatros with *Jasta* 11 he attacked six FE2ds of 20 Squadron, RFC. In the ensuing dogfight the observer of one of the FEs wounded the Red Baron in the head, causing him to break off combat and make a heavy landing near Wericq. After being hospitalised Richthofen returned to duty but was plagued with headaches and dizziness. Nevertheless he managed to fly and score victory after victory, and by 30 November 1917 he had shot down 63 enemy aircraft.

The Red Baron's last year, 1918, dawned and during March he shot down 11 aircraft, making his total 74. On 2 April, the Kaiser awarded him the last of his 26 decorations, the Order of the Red Eagle with Crowns and Swords. By 20 April he had achieved what was to be his final score, 80 confirmed victories. On Sunday, 21 April 1918 Manfred Freiherr von Richthofen, Rittmeister, the Red Baron, took off from his base at Cappy, France, with his *Jasta* 11 on what was to be his final flight. *Jasta* 11 engaged the enemy over Le Hamel and a huge dogfight ensued with the Red Baron in the thick of it. Richthofen swung onto the tail of a 209 Squadron Camel flown by a

*Officers from the Australian Flying Corps placing wreaths on the grave of Manfred von Richthofen.*

young pilot, Lieutenant Wilfred May, and gave chase. Captain A Roy Brown DSC, flying above, saw May's perilous position and dived to the rescue. Coming up on Richthofen's aircraft from behind Brown opened fire and scored a long burst on the all-red Triplane. Apparently unharmed, Richthofen continued to chase and machine-gun May's Camel.

As Richthofen flew low over Morlancourt Ridge he came under a hail of fire from Australian ground gunners beneath. Machine-gun fire raked the red Triplane and the gunners saw the Red Baron's head snap backwards in his cockpit. His aircraft sideslipped, then glided into the ground nose first. The Red Baron was dead, killed in action.

The following message was dropped by a British aircraft and was addressed to the German Flying Corps.

To,

The German Flying Corps.

Rittmeister Baron Manfred von Richthofen

was killed in aerial combat

on April 21st, 1918.

He was buried with full

military honours.

From British Royal Air Force.

Rittmeister Baron Manfred von Richthofen was buried with full military honours at Bertangles with his coffin draped with the

Imperial German Flag. Pilots of the German Army Air Service flew over his grave and dropped wreaths unhindered. His remains were returned to Berlin in 1925 and reburied at the Invaliden dome.

## Leutnant der Reserve Peter RIEPER
(1887–?)

Born on 13 April 1887 near Hannover, Rieper studied chemistry and qualified as a doctor in 1912. The following year he enlisted in the Army Reserve for the usual one year service, but in August 1914 transferred to the Regular Army, serving with the 74th Field Artillery Regiment with the rank of Vizewachtmeister. The regiment was soon in action and during one particularly heavy engagement he was wounded. On return to duty Rieper requested training as a balloon observer where his artillery training and experience could be put to good use. His request was granted and after training he qualified in the ultra dangerous balloon observer role.

*Portrait shot of Leutnant* der *Reserve Peter Rieper wearing his* Pour le Mérite.

Serving with *Ballonzug* 19 as an artillery spotter and intelligence gatherer, he quickly found out just how dangerous it was to be a balloon observer. Seated alone in a wicker basket slung under a tethered balloon, the brave observer made an easy target for enemy aircraft. His only contact with the ground was by telephone cable which often broke leaving the observer helpless. If attacked the observer could – if uninjured – make a quick exit by a static-line parachute attached to the basket.

In one such incident, on 17 October 1915, Rieper had to put all his nerve and skill to the test. He was at an altitude of 1,300 metres when he was told that two enemy fighters were on their way towards him. The ground crew opened fire with their revolving cannon known as a '*Lichtspucker*' (Light Spitter), but with little or no effect on the approaching aircraft. As an incendiary rocket punctured the balloon, Peter Rieper decided that it was time to leave and tightened his parachute belt. Swinging his legs over the side he lowered himself out of the basket and prepared to drop from the now blazing balloon, when he noticed that one of the parachute lines had snagged. Climbing hand over hand back into the basket, Rieper freed the line then plunged head first over the side. Seconds later as his parachute opened, the blazing balloon swept down past him, the heat searing him as it went.

By 1916 he was a Leutnant der Reserve Balloon Observer, but had a close call in the spring when his balloon was attacked by four enemy

*Leutnant der Reserve Peter Rieper preparing for an ascent in the basket of his observation balloon.*

Series of three photographs showing the precarious existence led by balloon observers.

Left: Sopwith Camel about to attack a Draken balloon.

Bottom left: Observer leaping from the balloon on a parachute after his balloon had been hit by gunfire.

Bottom right: The remains of his flaming balloon hurtling toward the ground.

fighters. Rieper was busy directing artillery fire on an enemy rail marshalling yard and failed to notice the approaching aircraft. Armed with only a Mauser rifle he returned fire but was no match for several machine-guns. Luckily for him the German ace Max Immelmann came to his rescue and saw off the enemy aircraft so that Rieper's accurate artillery spotting resulted in the marshalling yard being destroyed. However, fate caught up with the Leutnant on 3 June 1918 when aloft near Villers-Cotterêts. Allied gunfire opened up and his balloon began to burn, riddled with machine-gun fire. In the barrage of fire Rieper was badly wounded in the shoulder and decided to take to his parachute. Leaping from the doomed balloon with seconds to spare, he landed in front of German lines and was dragged along the ground by strong winds with such force that he broke his leg and suffered severe injuries. He was taken to hospital where his right arm was amputated and his leg put in plaster. After two months in hospital in Hamburg, he was declared unfit for further active service at the front and was posted to the *Luftschifferschule* in Namur as an instructor.

A month later, on 7 July 1918, for unstinting dedication to duty, he was awarded the *Pour le Mérite* – the only German balloon observer to be so honoured. He survived the war and went into business.

## Oberleutnant Friedrich Ritter von RÖTH
(1893–1918)

Born in Nurenberg on 29 September 1893 of a military family, Friedrich von Röth started his military career at the outbreak of war. He volunteered to join the 8th Bavarian Field Artillery Regiment, and because of his background was immediately promoted to Unteroffizier. In almost the first action in which his regiment was involved Röth was seriously injured, and spent almost a year in hospital, during which he received his commission as Leutnant on 29 May 1915. It was also at this time that he considered a career move to the German Army Air Service. After recuperating Röth applied for pilot training and after just a few weeks was severely injured again in a flying accident during training, which put him back in hospital for almost a year, but he was able to qualify as a pilot in February 1917.

Röth was assigned to FA(A) 296b on 1 April 1917 and carried out a number of reconnaissance sorties. In June 1917, he was awarded the Bavarian Military Merit Order 4th Class with Swords. Then began a series of moves to different *Jastas*: on 10 September he was posted to *Jastaschule* 1, then to *Jasta* 34 on 17 September and to *Jasta* 23 on 4 October. He was awarded the Iron Cross 1st Class on 1 November for his dedication to his role as a reconnaissance pilot. In January 1918 Röth changed from being a reconnaissance pilot and became an attacking, aggressive pilot when on 25 January, he attacked and shot down three reconnaissance balloons in one day, all within ten

*Oberleutnant Friedrich Ritter von Röth leaning against the wing of his Albatros D.III.*

*Oberleutnant der Reserve
Friedrich Ritter von Röth
(right) talking with
Hauptmann Ritter von
Schleich in front of Röth's
Albatros D.III.*

minutes of each other. For this dangerous mission he was to be awarded the Knight's Cross of the Military Max-Joseph Order. The granting of this award allowed Röth to use the title Ritter allowing his name to be changed to Friedrich Ritter von Röth. The following month, on 25 February, another award was given to him, the Knight's Cross with Swords of the Hohenzollern House Order.

On 24 April 1918 Röth took command of *Jasta* 16. By this time he had raised his tally to ten, nine of which were balloons, the other being an RE.8 of 16 Squadron, RFC. He was promoted to Oberleutnant on 19 August, and having reached the 'magic' number of 22 kills, was awarded the *Pour le Mérite* on 9 September. On the cessation of hostilities Röth's tally had risen to 28, of which 20 were observation balloons scored in multiples of two or three during probing expeditions over enemy lines.

At the end of the war Röth could not come to terms with Germany's defeat. He had been convinced that his country was invincible and that right was on its side throughout the conflict. On New Year's Eve 1918/19 at the age of 25, he committed suicide.

## Leutnant der Reserve Fritz RUMEY
(1891–1918)

Fritz Rumey was born in Königsberg, Bavaria, on 3 March 1891. After leaving school at 16 he became an apprentice roof slater, then in 1911 he volunteered to join Infantry Regiment Nr.45 as an infantryman. Three years later, at the outbreak of the First World War, his regiment was mobilised and sent to the Russian Front. Rumey was detached to the 3rd Grenadier Regiment and was immediately in action. In the following 12 months he distinguished himself sufficiently to be awarded the Iron Cross 2nd Class, but it was not long before he realised that there was another kind of war going on – the war in the air.

At the beginning of 1915 Fritz Rumey volunteered for transfer to the German Army Air Service and on 5 August he was posted to the flying school at Hundsfeld near Breslau. After training and gaining his badge and certificate he was posted to FA(A) 219 as an observer. After more than a year of flying as an observer on reconnaissance missions Rumey applied for training as a pilot, and was posted to *Jastaschule* on the Western Front early in 1917.

On completion of his training Rumey was posted to *Jasta* 2 in May

*Portrait shot of Leutnant Fritz Rumey just prior to his being awarded the Pour le Mérite.*

1917, and then to *Jasta* 5 on the 10 June with the rank of Vizefeldwebel. At the end of June he was promoted again and commissioned in the rank of Leutnant, which he celebrated by opening his tally on 26 June when he shot down the British ace Lieutenant E C Eaton of 65 Squadron. For this he received the Bavarian Militery Merit, 2nd Class with Swords on 7 July. During one combat mission against the British, on 25 August 1917, he was wounded and only just managed to get himself and his aircraft back to his field, but after two weeks he was back in the air adding to his tally, and by the end of the year had raised it to five.

By the end of May 1918 Rumey's tally had mounted to 21 and he had been awarded the Golden Military Merit Cross. His efforts had not gone unnoticed and with his tally at 29 he was awarded Germany's most prestigious award, the *Orden Pour Le Mérite*, making him one of only five airmen to be awarded both the *Pour le Mérite* <u>and</u> the Golden Military Merit Cross.

Fritz Rumey continued to wreak havoc amongst the British squadrons until 27 September 1918, when in the midst of a dogfight over Neuville St Remy, the top wing of his Fokker D.VII collided with the wing of an SE5a flown by Captain G E B Lawson of 32 Squadron, RAF. With his aircraft spinning towards the ground Fritz Rumey took to his parachute but it failed to deploy and he was killed. Captain Lawson, on the other hand, managed to guide his badly damaged SE5a to the ground and survived. Fritz Rumey was 27 years old.

### Oberleutnant zur See Gotthard SACHSENBERG
(1891–1961)

Gotthard Sachsenberg was born on 6 December 1891 in Rosslau, the son of a wharf owner. His early years, like so many others, were uneventful until in 1913, at the age of 22, he joined the Imperial German Navy as a sea cadet, spending part of the first year at sea aboard the battleship *Pommern*. A year later Germany was at war and almost immediately Sachsenberg volunteered for aviation duties in the newly formed German Naval Air Service. Like others before him he wanted to be a pilot, but the need for observers was just as great. After training he was posted to Marine FA 2, where after ten missions he was awarded the Iron Cross 2nd Class as a Fahnrich (Officer Cadet). Then in January 1916 his commission as Leutnant came through, and with it a new posting to training school, this time as an instructor. In the meantime Sachsenberg had applied for pilot training which was approved, whereupon he was posted to *Jastaschule* at Mannheim for training in February 1916, and after graduating in April returned to his old unit, Marine FA 2, flying Fokker E.IIIs from Mariakerke.

Sachsenberg had no success as a fighter pilot that year mainly because of a lull in the fighting in his area, but he continued to carry out observation duties. Then in May 1917, after having taken command of MFJI in the February, the fighting suddenly escalated and he scored his first victory, a Belgian Henri Farman over Dixmude. On 20 August, with six victories, he received the Knight's Cross with Swords of the Hohenzollern House Order. By the end of 1917 he had raised his tally to eight and was awarded the Iron Cross 1st Class, House Order of Albert the Bear and the Knight's 1st Class with Swords. The beginning of 1918 saw the war again intensifying; by the end of August Sachsenberg's tally had risen to 24 and he was awarded the *Pour le Mérite*. Other honours came his way with the Friedrich Cross 1st and 2nd Class of Anhalt, Friedrich-August Cross 1st and 2nd Class of Oldenburg and the Hanseatic Cross of Hamburg. At the end of the war his tally stood at 31.

Sachsenberg was given the task at the beginning of 1919 of forming a *Marine Freikorps*, MJGrI, for operations in the Baltic. He collected 50 officers, 650 ground crew and 70 aircraft and headed for the airfield at Riga. Fighter Squadron 'Sachsenberg', as it was known, became very successful, but within seven months political pressure

*Portrait shot of Oberleutnant zur See Gotthard Sachsenberg wearing his Pour le Mérite.*

*Oberleutnant zur See Gotthard Sachsenberg with two friends. L–R: Carl Jacobs; Gotthard Sachsenberg; Theodor Osterkamp, leaning against the Jasta staff car.*

was brought to bear on Reichswehr Minister Noske to withdraw the squadron, and in December 1919 the squadron was disbanded and recalled to Germany. Sachsenberg continued in the field of aviation and was one of those who was responsible for the development of air traffic control in Germany. He also became heavily involved in the social-political issues of the time and in 1920 wrote a thesis called 'On the Way to a Working Peace'. A rather unprophetic statement in view of what was to happen some years later.

Oberleutnant zur See Gotthard Sachsenberg died on 23 August 1961 at the age of 70.

## Leutnant Karl Emil SCHÄFER
(1891–1917)

Karl Emil Schäfer was born on 17 December 1891 in Kregfeld-Bockum, Bavaria, the son of a silk cloth manufacturer. In 1909 he served a year's compulsory service in the Army with the 10th *Jäger* Regiment. After leaving the Army Schäfer went to Paris and was there when the First World War broke out. Despite some difficulties he managed to return to Germany and was almost immediately assigned to the 7th *Jäger* Reserve Regiment which went into action within weeks of his joining and in the September he won the Iron Cross 2nd Class and promotion to Vizefeldwebel. Within days of receiving the award and the promotion he was badly wounded during an attack and was hospitalised for six months. It was whilst in hospital that he considered a move to the German Army Air Service. On release from hospital he rejoined his unit and soon after, in May 1916, was granted a commission as Leutnant and was awarded the Iron Cross 1st Class and the Military Merit Order 4th Class with Swords from Bavaria. He then asked to be transferred to the German Army Air Service for training as a pilot. This was approved and after only two months training at the flying school at Köslin he was awarded his pilot's badge and certificate.

On 30 July 1916 Schäfer was sent to the Eastern Front where he joined KG 2, *Staffel* 8, and over the next six months he flew more than 50 reconnaissance and bombing missions. During the battles around the area of Wolhynien, Schäfer dropped over 5,000 lbs of bombs, inflicting heavy casualties on the Russians. Then his unit was moved to the Western Front and Schäfer joined *Kasta* II of KG.3. On 22 January he scored his first victory when he shot down a French Caudron over west Pont-à-Mousson. It was to be the start of a rapid but short career. He was posted to join Manfred von Richthofen's *Jasta* 11 on 21 February 1917 and made his mark by shooting down

*Portrait of Leutnant Karl Schäfer wearing the ribbon of the Iron Cross 2nd Class.*

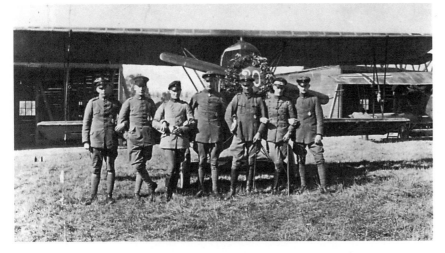

*Pilots from Jasta 15. Third from left is Karl Schäfer wearing the ribbon of the Iron Cross 2nd Class.*

*Leutnant Karl Schäfer in the cockpit of his Albatros D.III.*

eight aircraft in the following month of March, five of them in two days. By the end of April he had raised his tally to 23 and had been awarded the Knight's Cross with Swords of the Hohenzollern House Order and the nation's most prestigious award, the *Pour le Mérite*. He was also given command of *Jasta* 28. During the following month of May Schäfer raised his tally to 29 and on 4 June he shot down a DH.4 from 55 Squadron, RFC, bringing his tally to 30. Just after 4 p.m. on 5 June 1917 he and other members of *Jasta* 28 engaged FE2d fighters of 20 Squadron, RFC. After a short but vicious fight Schäfer was shot down and killed by an FE2d, A6469, flown by Lieutenant H L Satchell and his observer T A Lewis. Karl Schäfer was 26 years old.

### Hauptmann Eduard Ritter von SCHLEICH – 'The Black Knight'
(1888–1945)

Eduard Schleich was born in Munich, Bavaria, on 9 August 1888. Little is known of his early life, but his military career began in 1908 when he joined the 11th Bavarian Infantry Regiment as a Fähnrich (cadet). Two years later he received his commission and was placed on the reserve list. In 1914 he was called up to join his old regiment and within months was in the thick of the action. On 25 August 1914 he was severely wounded and was returned to Munich to recuperate and convalesce. It was while convalescing that he decided upon a career change and applied to be transferred to the German Army Air Service. He was accepted and in May 1915 was posted to FEA 1 at Schliessheim for training. On 11 September 1915, on completion of his flying training, he was awarded his Bavarian pilot's badge. It is important to note that it was the Bavarian pilot's badge that he was awarded as this was to be the cause of certain problems later.

Schleich's first posting was to FA 2b in October 1915 and after a number of reconnaissance flights he was wounded during an encounter with Allied fighters in February 1916. In September 1916, after recuperating, he was suddenly and unexpectedly put in command of *Fliegerschule* I where he became a flying instructor. Early in February 1917 he was transferred to a Bavarian escort unit, *Schutzstaffel* 28, as its commanding officer. His delight did not last long because, as there was a shortage of aircraft, he was unable to lead his unit but had to 'fly' a desk. Within weeks he had written furious letters to KoF1 (Fifth Army) headquarters requesting that he be transferred to a fighter unit. Although he had been an instructor he was posted to fighter training school at Famars, near Valenciennes. His instructor, Leutnant Boehme, announced after two weeks' instruction, that he could teach him no more and suggested that he be sent to a fighter unit.

He was posted to *Jasta* 21 on 21 May 1917 with the rank of Oberleutnant and again given command of the squadron, albeit only temporarily, without having won a single victory. However, he scored his first one on 25 May when, whilst on patrol over Moronvillers, he

*Portrait of Hauptmann Eduard Ritter von Schleich wearing his* Pour le Mérite.

shot down a Spad V.II. For a first victory this was a notable one for his opponent was none other than the French ace Sous-Lieutenant René Pierre Marie Dorme, who at the time had 43 victories to his credit. Dorme's gold watch was later dropped over a French airfield, together with a note from *Jasta* 21, saying that Dorme had died bravely for France.

After his second victory on 17 June, a Sopwith 1½-Strutter, Schleich was given command of the squadron permanently and it was then that the problems started. It has to be remembered that there still existed in Germany a feudal system and the fact that

*Jasta* 21 was a Prussian unit that had just been redesignated a Saxon unit, and which was now being commanded by a Bavarian, became what can only be described as a source of embarrassment to the senior Prussian members of the old military guard who still held positions of high authority in the German military machine. Schleich's command was put under the microscope and any infringement, no matter how minor, was leapt upon by the powers-that-be.

Over the following four months Schleich raised his tally to 25, but his command came under attack for the lack of results from his other pilots. After one escapade concerning three of his pilots, which got him a severe reprimand, he assembled all the pilots together and threatened that unless they showed more offensive spirit they would be removed from the squadron in disgrace. Within days the pilots starting scoring victories and the pressure from above eased, although this success was not without its losses. In the July the squadron had moved to Chassogne-Ferme near Verdun, and during one skirmish with the enemy Schleich's friend Leutnant Limpert was killed. Out of respect for his friend Schleich had his Albatros D.Va painted jet black. The black fighter with its white band around the fuselage became well known to Allied fighter pilots and soon earned Schleich the name 'The Black Knight'.

Schleich, although a commanding officer, was not immune to his own foolish lapses. One such incident happened after a Spad had been forced down intact. Schleich had the aircraft painted in

*Pilots from Jagdgeschwader 4, L–R: Leutnant Freytag; Leutnant Stark; Ritter von Schleich as Oberleutnant; Leutnant Seywald.*

German markings and headed for the front where he actually joined up with a French squadron on patrol. It took several minutes before the French pilots realised what was happening, but before they could react Schleich had headed back for his own lines only to be fired upon by German anti-aircraft fire. Fortunately their aim was poor and he landed back safely at his own airfield. KoF1 was not amused and severely reprimanded him for the escapade.

The rest of the squadron was performing well. Among them were Leutnant Emil Thuy and Leutnant Karl Thom, who were both later awarded the *Pour le Mérite*. Just after achieving his 25th victory Schleich fell ill to dysentery and was rushed to hospital in a serious condition. Some months later he was told that Prussian bureaucracy had taken advantage of his enforced absence and had him removed, as they decreed that no Bavarian should serve in a Prussian unit, let alone command one. It was at times like these when one wonders who the Germans were actually fighting!

On 23 October 1917 Schleich was given command of *Jasta* 32, an all-Bavarian squadron, his tally by this time having risen to 35. He was awarded the *Pour le Mérite* on 4 December 1917 in recognition of his services by the King of Prussia, but did not receive the customary Hohenzollern House Order that usually accompanied it.

The following month he was given command of *Jastaschule* 1 and in March 1918 command of *Jagdgruppe* Nr.8 which consisted of Bavarian *Jastas* 23, 34 and 35. It was not until the end of 1918 that he learned that he had been awarded the Knight's Cross of the Military Max Joseph Order, the Saxon Knight's Cross, the Albrecht Order 2nd Class and the Bavarian Military Merit Order 4th Class with Crown and Swords. With these awards came promotion to Hauptmann and the title of nobility, Eduard Ritter von Schleich. He remained in control of *Jagdgruppe* 8 until the end of the war, which he completed by being a member of the Armistice Committee.

In the 1920s he joined Lufthansa and stayed until the rise of Nazism, when he joined the Luftwaffe in 1933. He even visited Britain in the black uniform of the Waffen SS. Schleich fought in the Spanish Civil War as a member of the 'Condor Legion' and was one of those instrumental in bringing General Franco to power. During the Second World War he rose to the rank of Generaloberst commanding combat units. He later took up a post in occupied Denmark, before becoming General der Fliegers in Norway. He was taken prisoner at the end of the war by the Allies and interned in a prisoner-of-war camp for high ranking officers. It was there that he died following a short illness in 1945.

### Leutnant Wilhelm Paul SCHREIBER
(?–1918)

Of all the awards of the *Pour le Mérite*, the one to Leutnant Wilhelm Paul Schreiber has to be the most unusual. The usual practice of the Prussians was that the award was only made to officers who were alive, but <u>never</u> posthumously, yet Schreiber had died whilst his award was still being processed. What made him different is not known, although some say the award was given as an incentive to others to follow. But there were other aviators who had been recommended for the award and who had died before they could receive it, and their names were never put on the list of holders of the *Pour le Mérite*. Consequently, although Schreiber was technically given the award, the *Orden Pour le Mérite* itself was never actually presented to his family.

*Portrait of Leutnant Wilhelm Paul Schreiber.*

Little is known of Wilhelm Paul Schreiber prior to his joining the Army, but at the outbreak of the First World War he joined up as an artilleryman. Schreiber served on all the major fronts for the first two years of his career, earning himself the Iron Cross 2nd Class. Then in October 1916 he applied for transfer to the German Army Air Service and was sent for evaluation as an observer to *Armee Flugpark* 1. At the beginning of November 1916 it was decided to make use of his natural observation skills and he was posted to the observers' school at Königsberg in East Prussia.

Paul Schreiber finished the normal six-month course in three months. How he completed the course in such a short time, or whether the fatality rate of observers at the front warranted its speeding up, is not known. On 14 February 1917 he was assigned to *Flieger-Abteilung* (A) 221 on operational duties over the Somme. The very next day he was introduced to his pilot, Unteroffizier Heinrich-Ernst Schäfer, and almost immediately they were flying low-level reconnaissance and infantry support missions. Their first mission was nearly their last when they were jumped by ten British fighters and their Albatros was raked with machine-gun fire, forcing them to make an emergency landing. Over the next couple of months the team of Schreiber and Schäfer completed numerous reconnaissance and support sorties, including one bombing raid on a British airfield near Bailleul where they dropped 25 small bombs. For this daring and dangerous aerial attack Schreiber was awarded the Iron Cross 1st Class and Schäfer was promoted to Vizefeldwebel.

Throughout the following year Schreiber and Schäfer carried out similar missions, seemingly flying lower and lower in their armour-plated Albatros. On 7 March 1918 their efforts were recognised and Schreiber's observation role was rewarded by the award of the Knight's Cross with Swords of the Hohenzollern House Order. Two weeks later, on another low-level mission, their Albatros was hit by armour-piercing bullets and their fuel tank ruptured, causing them to carry out an emergency landing. This time the aircraft was badly damaged and was replaced with an armour-plated Junkers J.1, No. 134/17.

The German Army made its big push in April 1918 and Schreiber and Schäfer continued to fly longer and lower missions, bringing back vital troop movement and artillery spotting information. For their unstinting bravery in providing so much valuable information Schreiber was put forward for the *Pour le Mérite*, and Schäfer for the NCO's equivalent, the Golden Military Merit Cross. Then on 30 May the inevitable happened when, flying at treetop height, their Junkers J.1 was hit by withering fire from the ground. Schäfer was hit in the head and the aircraft went out of control, crashing into the ground with tremendous force. Both men were killed and it was discovered later that their aircraft had taken over 200 hits during this action.

Both men's awards were approved by the Kaiser and although Schäfer's family received his Golden Military Merit Cross, Schreiber's family did not receive his *Pour le Mérite*, although they received instead a letter from the commander of 17 *Armee*, which said:

*Leutnant Wilhelm Paul Schreiber (left) with Vizefeldwebel Heinrich-Ernst Schäfer.*

The exceptionally vigorous spirit, the constantly driving forward characteristics of the fallen fighter which he displayed time and time again on numerous missions over the lines and which led to his great accomplishments, were the determining factors in the Supreme Commander's recommending your son for the highest of all awards, the *Orden Pour le Mérite*. It is an honour-laden duty for me to tell you that it has pleased His Majesty, the Emperor and King, on June 8 to award your son the high *Orden Pour le Mérite*.

Under the regulations, unfortunately, there can be no transmittal of the high award if the bestowal of the award has been made posthumously. May it, however, be of some consolation to you in your great sorrow that your son, who fell as a brave hero for his Fatherland, was considered deserving of the highest of all recognition by the Supreme War Lord because of his outstanding service.

## Fregattenkapitän Peter STRASSER
(1876–1918)

Born on 1 April 1876 in Hannover, Peter Strasser was to follow in the naval traditions of his family. After leaving school Strasser joined the Navy as a cadet at the age of 15. He received his initial training on the training ships *Stein* and *Moltke* and upon graduating was sent to the Navy School in Kiel. Further training on the specialised training ships *Mars* and *Blücher* in gunnery completed his training and he was promoted to Leutnant zur See.

In 1897 Strasser was posted to the cruiser *Hertha* and toured East Asia for two years. He returned to a shore base before being posted again to the gunboat *Panther* as gunnery officer from 1902 to 1904. After a period at a shore base Strasser was posted to the battleship *Westfalen*, where his skill as a gunnery officer was proven when he won the *Kaiserpreis* for the best gunnery officer in the service. Strasser, a dedicated professional seaman, was a fair but strict disciplinarian, and his gunnery crews were amongst the best. In 1910 he was posted to the battleship *Mecklenburg*, where his reputation went before him. He won the *Kaiserpreis* for the next three years, during which time he had applied for a transfer to the aviation wing. This had been refused on the grounds that he was too valuable a gunnery officer to be lost to the new aviation wing. Then in September 1913 it all changed.

*Fregattenkapitän Peter Strasser in the gondola of a Zeppelin with Count von Zeppelin (wearing the flat cap).*

Strasser was ordered to report to naval headquarters in Berlin on 1 September 1913. After reporting to the adjutant he was shown into the office of a senior naval officer. After hearing a breakdown of his career read out to him, he was told of the demise of Leutnantkommander Matzing in the crash of Zeppelin L1 in the North Sea and was then told that he was to be put in command of naval Zeppelins. Strasser pleaded that he had no knowledge of airships, but it was pointed out to him that all the most experienced airship men had died in the crash and new men had to be trained. It was a dedicated disciplinarian that the Navy wanted, knowing full well it was also going to need an officer of strength of character to carry this off.

Less than a month after taking command his temperament was put to the test when airship L2 exploded in mid-air, killing all the crew. By interrogating all the witnesses Strasser found the cause and arranged for modifications to be made to the one existing airship and all future ones. At the outbreak of war in 1914 the Naval Air Division found itself with just one airship, the L3. Strasser immediately requested the building of new ones, pointing out to the High Command the advantage of being able to fly above any blockade the British may impose and bomb London from the air.

On 19 January 1915 the first raid on Britain took place. The L6, carrying Strasser, and the L3 and L4, lifted off shortly before 11 a.m. Not long after take-off the L6 had to return due to engine trouble, but the remaining two attacked the Norfolk region of Britain and

*The Zeppelin L70 in which Fregattenkapitän Peter Strasser lost his life when it was shot down whilst on a bombing mission.*

*Portrait of Fregattenkapitän Peter Strasser in naval uniform wearing his* Pour le Mérite.

bombed Great Yarmouth. Although very little damage was done, the fact that Britain had been bombed from the air made the British painfully aware that they were no longer impregnable. Strasser was promoted to Korvettenkapitän for his part in the organisation and partial success of the raid and from this meagre beginning he was to build a fleet of airships that carried out over 200 sorties and over 1,000 reconnaissance flights against the Allies. Strasser was promoted to Fregattenkapitän on 20 August 1917 and was awarded Germany's highest honour, the *Pour le Mérite*. He continued to lead his men in the attacks against Britain, and on 5 August 1918 he led the entire squadron of airships on a raid over London. As they approached Yarmouth, Strasser, in the biggest and newest airship, the L70, suddenly saw an aircraft, a DH.4 flown by Lieutenant Peter Cadbury RNAS, appear out of the dense cloud in front of them. The guns of the DH.4 suddenly opened up and incendiary and tracer bullets ripped into the gas bags and fuel tanks of the L70. Strasser and his crew were helpless as flames spurted from the sides of the giant airship, then seconds later it exploded in a mass of burning fuel and tangled metal. The remains of the giant airship and its crew plunged into the dark waters of the North Sea that were to become their grave. The remaining airships, on seeing that they had been discovered, aborted their mission and returned to Nordholz. In four short years Peter Strasser had taken an idea and turned it into reality – to disrupt Britain's way of life during the war years in a manner that had never been dreamed of, and in doing so occupy thousands of soldiers and hundreds of pieces of artillery in trying to combat the new threat. Peter Strasser certainly left his mark on military history.

## Leutnant Karl THOM

(1893–?)

Born on 19 May 1893 in Freystadt, West Prussia, Karl Thom was just one of the many young men whose life was altered dramatically by war. After leaving school at the age of 14 he had a succession of jobs until he was 18, then in 1911 he joined the Army, volunteering for three years' military service, and was assigned to the 5th Hussar Regiment. Three years later war broke out and Thom, now an experienced soldier, was posted to the Jäger Regiment *Pferde* Nr.10 on 4 September 1914 and promoted to Unteroffizier. The regiment was soon in action, and in one particularly unpleasant fight Thom was

*Portrait of Leutnant Karl Thom.*

seriously injured for which he received the Iron Cross 2nd Class. After being released from hospital in June 1915 he applied for transfer to the German Army Air Service and was accepted.

In the September Thom was sent to pilot training school where, in January 1916, he graduated as a pilot. He was posted to FA 216 which was operating patrols in the Vosges sector, where he carried out reconnaissance missions. On 16 May 1916 he crashed on landing and was badly injured. On release from hospital Thom was promoted to Vizefeldwebel on 24 July and was posted to Romania in October to join FA 48 as a reconnaissance pilot. At the end of October he was shot down and captured but managed to escape and made his way back to his unit. For

*Leutnant Karl Thom with two fellow pilots: Luthringer (left); Schmückle (centre) and Thom (right).*

Werkm. Luthringer, Schmückle, Thom (27 vict. P.l.)

this he was awarded the Iron Cross 1st Class. Thom yearned for more action and a chance to go hunting himself instead of continually being the hunted. On 24 April, after a number of requests, he was posted to *Jastaschule* and trained as a fighter pilot. On graduation on 15 May he was posted to *Jasta* 21.

Karl Thom opened his score on 22 August 1917 when he shot down a French AR2 whilst on patrol over south Avocourt. Two weeks later he scored again when he shot down a Caudron whilst over Forêt de Hesse. At the end of September his tally had risen to 12, and he was awarded the Golden Military Service Cross. Thom had added two more kills to his tally, when on 23 December he attacked a balloon and was injured when set upon by defending Allied fighters. He managed to get his crippled aircraft back to his field and was hospitalised for a month as a result of his injuries. He returned to *Jasta* 21 on 24 January 1918 and was promoted to Offiziersstellvertreter. His tally remained static for several months as there appeared to be little action, but in June activity in the area became intense. By the beginning of August he had raised his tally to 27 and was awarded the Members' Cross with Swords of the Hohenzollern House Order. Four days later he was wounded again, only this time severely, when his patrol ran into SE5s from the RFC.

At the end of August he was given a commission in the rank of Leutnant, but was still in hospital and remained there until the beginning of October. On 1 November, five days before he again returned to *Jasta* 21, he was awarded the prestigious *Pour le Mérite*, making him one of only five airmen to be awarded both the *Pour le Mérite* <u>and</u> the Golden Military Service Cross. Thom stayed with *Jasta* 21 until the Armistice but again bad luck dogged him when he was badly injured in a crash the day before the war ended.

There are two versions of what happened to Karl Thom after the First World War. The first was that during the Second World War he joined the Luftwaffe and held posts in Eastern Germany. He was reported missing whilst visiting the Russian Front, is thought to have been taken prisoner and was never seen again.

The second was that the crash at the end of the First World War broke his back and he returned to Freystadt. There, it is said, he devoted his time to land settlement in Königsberg, where he later became Director of Programmes.

## Leutnant Emil THUY
(1894–1930)

Born on 11 March 1894 in Hagen, Westphalia, Emil Thuy was the son of a local schoolteacher. The early part of his life was uneventful, but like many others it was to be completely changed in 1914 by the outbreak of war. Emil Thuy was one of the first in his town to volunteer for front-line duty and was duly enlisted in the 3rd Rhineland Pioneer Regiment. Almost immediately, after very basic training, his regiment was sent to the Western Front. In October 1914, not long after the outbreak of war, Emil Thuy was badly wounded in action and was returned to Germany. Whilst in hospital it was soon realised that he was unfit for further active service at the front and he was discharged from the Army.

On his release Emil Thuy applied for the German Army Air Service and was accepted. On completion of his training he was awarded his certificate and pilot's badge and on 10 July 1915 was posted to FFA 53 as a reconnaissance pilot with the rank of Gefreiter. He was awarded the Iron Cross 2nd Class on 7 August, probably for his previous war experiences. After further combat training he scored his first victory on 8 September and was promoted to Unteroffizier later the same month. Thuy was awarded the Iron Cross 1st Class on 10 November, followed by promotion to Vizefeldwebel the following month, but it was not until 26 March 1917 that he received his commission as a Leutnant. Then in the November his request for fighter pilot training was granted and he was sent to *Jastaschule*. On graduating on 28 January 1917 Thuy was posted to *Jasta* 21. He opened his tally on 16 April when he shot down a Caudron whilst on patrol over north Berry-au-Bac. His tally had risen to 15 by 24 September and on 26 September he was made commander of *Jasta* 28. Emil Thuy was awarded the Knight's Cross with Swords of the Hohenzollern House Order on 6 November.

*Leutnant Emil Thuy standing alongside his Fokker D.VII at Jasta 21.*

By the end of 1917 his tally had risen to 17. On 2 February 1918, whilst on patrol, he and his flight were attacked by Allied fighters and, although wounded, Thuy was able to make his way back to his

*Portrait of Leutnant Emil Thuy wearing the ribbon of the Iron Cross 2nd Class.*

field. The wounds hospitalised him for several weeks, but on 21 February he was back in command of the *Jasta*. By the end of May he had raised his tally to 21 and was awarded the Knight's Cross of the Military Merit Order of Württemberg. On 6 June 1918 he became the leader of *Jagdgruppe* Nr.7 which consisted of *Jastas* 28, 33, 57 and 58 and on 30 June he was awarded Germany's highest award, the *Pour le Mérite*.

At the end of the war Emil Thuy remained in aviation, training pilots at flying schools. But as the Luftwaffe began to form, he became an instructor at a Luftwaffe flying school near Smolensk, Russia, and was killed on 11 June 1930 in a flying training accident.

## Hauptmann Adolf Ritter von TUTSCHEK
(1891–1918)

*Portrait of Oberleutnant Adolf Ritter von Tutschek wearing his Pour le Mérite.*

Adolf von Tutschek was born in Ingolstadt, Bavaria, on 16 May 1891. Both his father and grandfather were military men so it was natural that in 1910, at the age of 19, he joined the 3rd Bavarian Infantry Regiment as a cadet, and after serving his time he was commissioned in 1912. When the war broke out he was assigned to the 40th Bavarian Infantry Regiment and immediately was in action on the Western Front. One year later saw his regiment in action on the Eastern Front where he was wounded on 2 May. For this and other actions with which he had been involved he was awarded the Iron Cross 1st Class and the Bavarian Military Merit Order 4th Class with Swords. He was discharged from hospital in June and within days was back in action with his regiment. On 15 August he was awarded the Military Max Joseph Order which gave him the title of Ritter. He was recalled to headquarters on 17 January 1916 and promoted to Oberleutnant, then ordered back to the Western Front at Verdun. It was here that he was gassed on 26 March 1916 and it was while lying in hospital for several months that his thoughts turned to other ways of enhancing his military career. One of the services that

*Oberleutnant Adolf Ritter von Tutschek preparing to start his Fokker Dr.I at Foulis, where he was the OC of JG II.*

intrigued him was the German Army Air Service so he applied for a transfer and was accepted, although his own regiment was not at all keen on losing such an experienced infantry officer. Adolf Ritter von Tutschek reported to Schliessheim as a student pilot on 25 July 1916 and three months later at the end of October 1916, after qualifying as a pilot, he was posted to FA 6b to train as a single-seater pilot.

Another award caught up with him on 17 January 1917 when he was awarded the Bavarian Military Merit Order 4th Class with Crown and Swords. On completion of his single-seater training he was posted to *Jasta* 2 (Boelcke) on 25 January. In just over a month he had opened his score and raised his tally to three. At the end of April 1917 he was given command of *Jasta* 12, not only for his flying prowess and record, but because of the experience he had had in command of an infantry company. By the middle of July he had raised his tally to 13, for which he was awarded the Knight's Cross with Swords of the Hohenzollern House Order. In less than two months his tally had risen to 21 and he was awarded the coveted *Pour le Mérite* on 3 August 1917.

A week later, whilst on patrol, Tutschek came under attack from aircraft of No.8 Naval Squadron. He was severely wounded in the ensuing dogfight and was shot down by Flight Commander C D Booker, but he survived the crash and after recuperating was promoted on 6 December 1917 to Hauptmann. He was given command of the newly formed *Jagdgeschwader* Nr.II, made up of *Jastas* 12, 13, 15 and 19, on 1 February 1918, but it was to be a short-lived command. On 15 March 1918, whilst flying in his all-over green Fokker Dr.I No.404/17, he was shot down and killed by Lieutenant H B Redler of 24 Squadron, flying in his SE5a. Tutschek was 27 years old when he died and had 27 victories to his credit.

### Oberleutnant Ernst UDET

(1896–1941)

Probably one of the most charismatic German pilots of the First World War, Ernst Udet was born in Frankfurt-am-Main on 26 April 1896, the son of a wealthy landowner. Udet had a natural flair for anything mechanical and had his own motorcycle. He applied to join the Army at the age of 17, but was rejected several times before he was finally able to persuade the authorities to accept him. When on 7 August 1914 German troops occupied Liège, Ernst Udet reported to the German Automobile Club with his motorcycle to play his part as a messenger. On 21 August 1914 he joined the Army and was assigned to the 26th Württemberg Reserve Division as a motorcycle messenger.

*Portrait of Oberleutnant Ernst Udet wearing his* Pour le Mérite.

For the next few months Udet rode his motorcycle backwards and forwards behind the German lines delivering messages. Then on one particularly bad night, when the sound of guns appeared to be encircling him, he swerved to miss a shell hole in the road and crashed. After ten days in hospital he was sent to Belgium to catch up with his division but could not find them. In Liège he was given the job of delivering messages, and it was there that he met Leutnant von Waxheim, a pilot who was to influence Udet's life.

Orders came for Udet to be sent home but on arriving there he immediately volunteered for the Pilot's Reserve Detachment in Schliessheim. His meeting with von Waxheim had convinced him that this was where his future lay. Whilst waiting for a response to his request, he trained as a pilot at his own expense, sending further applications to Darmstadt and Döberitz. A few weeks later orders came through for him to go to Darmstadt for pilot training. After completion of his training Udet was posted to FA(A) 206 as a Gefreiter. He was assigned Leutnant Bruno Justinus as his observer, and three weeks later, after a spell of patrols in which they never saw an Allied aircraft, they spotted a French monoplane attacking a railway station. As they approached they realised that the Frenchman was in trouble and was gliding towards the ground. Udet tucked in behind him and noticed that the aircraft had a gun mounted behind the propeller. The French aircraft, encouraged by Udet, made a forced landing and before the pilot could set fire to it he was captured by German soldiers. The pilot, it was discovered later, was Roland Garros and the capture of his aircraft together with the machine-gun and its interruptor gear intact was to alter the course of air-to-air fighting dramatically. Udet received the Iron Cross 2nd Class for the incident.

On 18 March 1916 Udet was posted to FA 68, which later became *Kek* Habsheim, and scored his first victory when he shot down a Farman F40 whilst defending Mühlhausen during a raid by French aircraft. It is claimed that he attacked 22 hostile aircraft flying on his own in his Fokker D.III, 356/16. On 28 September he was posted to *Jasta* 15 where by the end of the year he had raised his tally to two, a very ignominious start for someone who was to become one of Germany's highest scoring fighter aces. At the beginning of January 1917 he was awarded the Iron Cross 1st Class and at the end of the month he was commissioned as a Leutnant.

In May 1917 he recorded his sixth victory and requested a transfer to *Jasta* 37. This was agreed and he was posted on 19 June. Five months later Udet received a telegram saying that his friend Leutnant Gontermann had been killed and that he was to take command of *Jasta* 37. Two weeks after that he was awarded the Knight's Cross with Swords of the Hohenzollern House Order, for by this time he had raised his tally to 15 confirmed victories. On 23 March 1918 Udet was posted to *Jasta* 11 as commanding officer until 8 April. Three days before his 22nd birthday, a telegram arrived, which read:

His Majesty the Emperor has been gracious enough to bestow upon you the *Pour le Mérite* in recognition of the twenty planes shot down by you.

The next day he was given command of *Jasta* 4.

Udet's aircraft was a very distinctive Fokker D.VII with a red fuselage. The upper surfaces of the top wing had red and white candy

*Ernst Udet (left) and Leutnant Weingärten at Habsheim Kek standing in front of a Fokker E.III.*

stripes and written on the upper tail surface for any attacker from the rear to read was the inscription '*Du noch Nicht!*' (Not you yet!). Most of his aircraft also carried the initials of his fiancée – 'LO'. With his tally of victories standing at 40 he was shot down during a dogfight with a French Breguet but escaped with only slight injuries. As his aircraft spun earthwards, Udet scrambled out of the cockpit only to find that his parachute harness had caught on the control column. After struggling for what seemed an eternity, he broke free, his parachute opening barely 300 feet from the ground. He landed heavily in a shell hole and was rescued by German infantry.

In the following two months he raised his tally to 60 confirmed victories and was awarded the Lübeck Hanseatic Cross and the Hamburg Hanseatic Cross. Then on 26 September 1918, with his tally raised to 62, he was badly wounded in the thigh, putting an end to his combat flying days.

After the war Udet became a test pilot and a movie stunt pilot flying all over the world. At the onset of the Second World War he was persuaded to join the Luftwaffe and attained the rank of Generaloberst. Then on 17 September 1941 Ernst Udet died. The German propaganda machine announced that he had died whilst testing a new aeroplane and Hitler announced that he would be given a state funeral. In reality Udet had committed suicide, using an old Mexican six-shooter that had been given to him in Hollywood during his days as a stunt pilot in the movies. His position in the Luftwaffe had become untenable due in the main to political infighting and the fact that his position was being consistently undermined. He was buried with full military honours.

### Leutnant der Reserve Joseph VELTJENS
(1894–1943)

Joseph Veltjens was born on 2 June 1894 in the small village of Geldern, west of Duisberg, in Saxony. After leaving high school he went to the Technical College at Charlottenburg, Berlin, to study machine construction. At the outbreak of the First World War, Veltjens joined the Army, enlisting in the Kaiserin Augusta Guards Regiment Nr.4 on 3 August 1914. Three months later he was attached to the Lieb Grenadier Regiment Nr.8 and later transferred to the 8th *Korps Kraftwagen Kolonne*. During this period he received a number of rapid promotions culminating in August 1915 with the rank of Vizefeldwebel and the award of the Iron Cross 2nd Class.

At the end of October 1915 Veltjens applied for transfer to the German Army Air Service and was accepted. He was sent to flying school at Döberitz and at the end of December 1915 he was awarded his pilot's certificate and badge. Veltjens was posted to Johannisthal for further training and after graduating on 10 May 1916 he was posted to FA 23 as a reconnaissance pilot. After flying a large number of sorties, he was commissioned at the end of 1916 as Leutnant in recognition of his skills in this field of flying. At the beginning of 1917 Veltjens met Rudolf Berthold who persuaded him to apply to *Jastaschule* for training as a fighter pilot. He was accepted and on completion of the course was posted to *Jasta* 14. The following

*Portrait of Leutnant Joseph Veltjens wearing his* Pour le Mérite. *His Gold Wound Badge can be seen between his Iron Cross 1st Class and his pilot's badge.*

month, on 14 April, he scored his first victory by shooting down a Spad whilst patrolling over Craonne in his Albatros. With his tally at five, he was posted on 15 August to *Jasta* 18 where by the end of 1917 he had raised his score to nine and had been awarded the Knight's Cross 2nd Class with Swords from Saxony.

On 20 March 1918 Veltjens was posted to *Jasta* 15 where, on 18 May, he took command and celebrated by shooting down a French Breguet XIV bomber over Cauny. This brought his tally to 13, and with it came the Iron Cross 1st Class, the Albrecht Order and the Knight's Cross with Swords of the Hohenzollern House Order on 20 May. Veltjens continued to score victories freely, and by the end of August 1918 had raised his tally to 31. His efforts were recognised and he was awarded Germany's highest honour, the *Pour le Mérite*. At the end of the war Joseph Veltjens had a total of 35 kills to his credit.

In 1919 he joined the Volunteer Corps

Lüttwitz and the Gerstenberg Division to fight against the Spartacists in Berlin and Bremen, and was amongst those who were instrumental in overthrowing them.

During the Second World War Veltjens joined the Luftwaffe with the rank of Oberst. He flew transport aircraft and at one time was Göring's emissary to Finland. He died in 1943 when the Junkers Ju52 which he was flying was shot down over Yugoslavia by resistance fighters.

### Leutnant der Reserve Werner VOSS
(1897–1917)

The eldest son of an industrial dyer, Werner Voss was born in Krefeld on 13 April 1897. He was expected to follow in the family tradition and the trade of dyeing that had been in the Voss family for generations, but Werner Voss had other ideas, for he was to become involved in a trade concerned with another kind of dying, and one that was to see him meet his demise at the early age of 20.

Werner Voss was a member of the Krefeld Militia and liked nothing better than to wear the uniform of the Krefeld Hussars two evenings a week and for two months each summer. When war broke out he was assigned to the 11th Westphalian Hussar Regiment and sent to the French border in Lorraine. Within days of his regiment arriving there, France declared war on Germany and Voss found himself involved in the last battle in which the cavalry was to play a vital role. Elsewhere in Germany cavalry units were being disbanded as it was decided they were no longer any use, and the Hussars were being turned into infantrymen. Voss had no liking for this and applied for pilot training in the German Army Air Force. In August 1915 he was accepted, and as by this time he was considered a veteran, he was promoted to Unteroffizier and awarded the Iron Cross 2nd Class – at just 18 years old.

Voss was sent to pilot training school where it was soon discovered that he was a natural pilot, and on completion of his course in

*Portrait of Leutnant Werner Voss wearing his* Pour le Mérite.

*Werner Voss standing in front of his Fokker Dr.I Triplane with a 'Totem-pole' face caricatured on the cowling.*

February 1916 he was posted to FEA 7 as an instructor. One month later he was promoted to Vizefeldwebel and posted to *Kampfgeschwader* 4 initially as an observer, but on receipt of his pilot's badge he took over the controls of the Aviatik two-seater fighter/bomber. In September he was commissioned as a Leutnant and in November he was posted to *Jasta* 2 where he was to fly with the legendary Baron Manfred von Richthofen. One month later, after scoring two victories (a Nieuport Scout and DH.2) he was awarded the Iron Cross 1st Class. By the end of February 1917 his tally of victims had risen to 12 and in March he was awarded the Knight's Cross with Swords of the Hohenzollern House Order. Voss's desire and dedication to increase his score was never better demonstrated than on 27 March 1917 when, after a gruelling fight with a British fighter, Voss forced the other aircraft to crash. Because he wished to claim the victory and there was no one around to substantiate it, Voss landed alongside the wreckage of the downed fighter and recovered its machine-gun. He took off in a hail of bullets from advancing soldiers on the ground, waving to them in delight. Voss was fast becoming a household name in Germany and on 8 April 1917, with his tally now at 24, he was awarded the *Pour le Mérite*.

May 1917 saw Werner Voss posted to *Jasta* 5 where by the end of June he had taken his tally to 34. He was given command of *Jasta* 29 for the month of July and then posted to *Jasta* 14 as acting commander – he was just 20 years old. At the end of July he was appointed Staffelführer of *Jasta* 10, his tally now standing at 34. Voss was flying a Fokker Dr.I with the distinctive chrome yellow cowling of *Jasta* 10, only his had a face painted on it. During August and September Voss increased his tally to 48, but then on 23 September 1917 he became engaged in what was to become known later as one of the most famous dogfights of the war. Whilst on patrol he came across a flight of British SE5s from 56 Squadron, but unknown to him, and also unfortunately for him, the flight consisted of a number of top British aces, including McCudden, Rhys-Davids, Barlow, Muspratt, Cronyn, Childlaw-Roberts and Bowman. For over ten minutes Werner Voss, almost single-handed, fought the flight, inflicting damage, some serious, on all the aircraft. It was Lieutenant Arthur Rhys-Davids who finally managed to get on the tail of the elusive Voss and a burst from his machine-guns sent Voss's Fokker Triplane 103/17 plummeting to the ground. He was buried by British soldiers on the spot where he crashed. Major James McCudden said of Voss afterwards,

> His flying was wonderful, his courage magnificent and in my opinion he is the bravest German airman whom it has been my privilege to see fight.

Leutnant Werner Voss was just 20 years old.

### Hauptmann Franz WALZ

(1885–1945)

Franz Walz was born on 4 December 1885 in the small hamlet of Speyer, south of Mannheim, Bavaria. At the age of 20 he volunteered for the Army and joined the 8th Bavarian Infantry Regiment in Metz on 15 July 1905. It was soon realised that he was a natural leader of men and three years later, in 1908, he was promoted to Leutnant. His interests soon moved beyond the infantry to the newly created German Army Air Service and in 1912 Leutnant Franz Walz applied to be transferred to this service, a request that was approved some months later. Walz was posted to the German Army's flying school at Munich-Schliessheim where he graduated some four months later.

At the outbreak of war in 1914 Walz took command of the Bavarian FFA 3, a reconnaissance unit in the Alsace-Lorraine area and was promoted to Oberleutnant in November 1914. The following year he carried out over 200 reconnaissance sorties on the Western Front and was rewarded in December 1915 with command of *Kaghol* I's *Kampfstaffel* 2, a two-seater reconnaissance aircraft squadron. On 9

April 1916 Franz Walz opened his score when he shot down a French Caudron whilst on a reconnaissance patrol over Douaumont and increased his tally on 21 May when he shot down a Nieuport. By the end of June Walz had raised his tally to five and had flown over 300 reconnaissance sorties. On 29 July he shot down an EA but during a reconnaissance mission the next day was wounded in the foot and after managing to return to base he was hospitalised for the next few months.

On his return to *Kaghol* I on 5 September 1916 he was awarded the Knight's Cross with Swords of the Hohenzollern House Order. Franz Walz was then given command of *Jasta* 2 on 29 November, followed by promotion to Hauptmann on 20 January 1917. He increased his tally to seven on 14 May and was again posted to command *Jasta* 34 the following month. It soon became obvious that his skills were as a reconnaissance pilot, not a fighter pilot, so it was decided to utilise him elsewhere. On 25 August 1917 he was posted to take command of FA 304b in Palestine. Here, he and his squadron carried out reconnaissance flights, culminating

*Portrait of Hauptmann Franz Walz wearing his* Pour le Mérite.

*Hauptmann Franz Walz, the 'Eagle of Jericho', standing with the Kommandeur der Flieger Hauptmann Weyert, alongside an LVG C.IV of Flieger Abteilung 304b.*

on 22 July 1918 with him being awarded the Turkish Silver Liakat Medaille, and a month later, on 9 August, he was awarded Germany's most prestigious award, the *Pour le Mérite*. Although the award was usually associated with fighter pilots, it was given to Franz Walz for the 500 sorties he had successfully carried out. In the following month, on 15 September, he was awarded the Osmanie *Orden* 4th Class with Swords. This award, together with his Iron Crosses 2nd and 1st Class, three other Bavarian awards and one Austro-Hungarian decoration showed the respect felt for this man, even though he was not a household name in Germany.

Shortly after 15 September he was captured by the British when his aircraft was forced down and he was released on 1 December 1919 after the war had finished. Franz Walz returned to Germany and served with the Reichswehr and State Police. In 1939, at the onset of the Second World War, he joined the Luftwaffe and had reached the rank of Generalleutnant by 1 April 1944. He was captured by the Russians at the beginning of 1945 and died as a prisoner of war in Breslau, Silesia, in December 1945.

### Leutnant der Reserve Rudolf WINDISCH
(1897–1918)

Born in Dresden on 27 January 1897, Rudolf Windisch was one of the few German pilots who had not come from an upper-class background. He entered military service in 1912, joining the 177th Infantry Regiment and within weeks of the war starting, Windisch was wounded, though not seriously. He then applied, whilst on sick leave, to be transferred to aviation school, and on 22 January 1915 he was assigned to the Military Pilot's School at Leipzig-Lindenthal. On graduating on 10 June he was promoted to Unteroffizier and assigned to FEA 6 as an instructor, soon becoming bored with teaching although it was a responsible and safe post. He had already tasted action as an infantryman and had been wounded for his trouble, but now he wanted more. So Windisch applied for a combat posting and on 1 May 1916 was sent to FFA 62 as a reconnaissance pilot. His observer was Oberleutnant Maximillian von Cossel, and although they both came from totally different backgrounds, they became firm friends almost immediately. A month later the whole unit was moved to the Russian Front and it was not long before he had made his mark with a number of daring reconnaissance flights over the front for which he was awarded the Iron Cross 2nd Class together with promotion to Vizefeldwebel.

On 25 August he scored his first victory and opened up his tally by shooting down an observation balloon. For this he was awarded the Iron Cross 1st Class followed some weeks later by the award of the Prussian Crown Order 4th Class with Swords thus becoming the only pilot to receive the order during the war. The award rose out of a special mission carried out by Windisch and his observer von Cossel when on 2 October 1916 Windisch was to land his aircraft behind the Russian lines and drop off von Cossel, whose brief it was to blow up a strategic railway bridge near Rowno-Brody. The following day, 3 October, Windisch returned to pick up his observer,

*Portrait of Leutnant Rudolf Windisch wearing his full medals.*

the mission completed. For this extremely daring act, both men were presented to the Emperor on 18 October when Maximilian von Cossel was presented with the Knight's Cross with Swords of the Hohenzollern House Order, and Rudolf Windisch with the Crown Order 4th Class with Swords. They both also received awards from their respective home states: von Cossel, the Cross of Merit 3rd Class with Swords, and Windisch, the Cross of Honour with Swords.

*Portrait of Windisch whilst a Vizefeldwebel with Oberleutnant von Cossel.*

Windisch later received the Military Order of St Heinrich Medal in Silver from Saxony, their highest bravery award.

After a short leave Windisch was sent to KG 2 on the Western Front on 24 November and on 5 December he was commissioned in the rank of Leutnant. He continued reconnaissance patrols until 20 February when he was posted to *Jasta* 32 as a fighter pilot. After further training he started to make his mark on Allied fighters, with an AR2 on 18 September, followed by a Spad on 27 September, bringing his tally to three. His fourth victim, a Spad, on 1 November 1917, brought him the Knight's Cross 1st Class with Swords of the Albert Order from Saxony.

By the end of November Windisch's tally had risen to six, whereupon he was posted to *Jasta* 50 on 10 January 1918 for just two weeks, and then to *Jasta* 66 as commanding officer. By the end of May 1918 he had raised his tally to 22, during which time he was awarded the Knight's Cross with Swords of the Hohenzollern House Order, the Austrian-Hungarian Bravery Medal in Silver 2nd Class and the Saxon St Heinrich Medal in Gold. On the day of his 22nd victory, he himself was shot down and taken prisoner by the French. Under the assumption that he was a prisoner of war, the *Pour le Mérite* was awarded to him, but it was never collected.

When the war was finally over and the repatriation of prisoners commenced, efforts were made to locate Leutnant Windisch, but he was never seen again. The story of his disappearance is shrouded in mystery, the French saying that there was no record of a Rudolf Windisch ever being in a prison camp. There were a number of explanations suggested, including one that he was shot trying to steal a French aeroplane, but this was never confirmed. To this day the fate of Leutnant Rudolf Windisch continues to be a mystery, and one that may never be solved.

### Leutnant Kurt WINTGENS
(1894–1916)

The son of an army officer, Kurt Wintgens was born in Neustadt on 1 August 1894. At the age of 19 he became a cadet with *Telegraphen* Battalion Nr.2 in Frankfurt and was sent to the military academy at Heersfeld to start his career, when war broke out, whereupon he immediately rejoined his unit and was soon in action against Allied forces; by the end of 1914 he had been awarded the Iron Cross 2nd

Class. Aviation was becoming the new chal-
lenge amongst young German officers and
Kurt Wintgens was not slow to see the advan-
tages and excitement it had to offer. He
applied to be transferred to the aviation section and was accepted as an observer but,
because of his experience in telegraphy, was
attached to the AOK IX (Army Wireless
*Abteilung*). His first experiences were on the
Western Front, then Poland, then in March
1915 he was accepted for pilot training and
assigned to *Jastaschule* at Schwerin. This selec-
tion of Wintgens was unusual as he wore
glasses, but within four months he had qualified as a pilot, exhibiting exceptional skills
that had him immediately posted to a fighter
squadron, FFA 67 flying Fokkers then on to
FFA 6b. On 1 July 1915 he opened his tally

*Portrait of Leutnant Kurt Wintgens wearing his* Pour le Mérite.

when he shot down a Morane Parasol whilst on patrol east of
Luneville. The claim was unconfirmed but had it been verified it
would have been the first German fighter kill in history. A second
claim for another Morane Parasol on 4 July was also unconfirmed.

Four days later he was posted to FFA 48 and ostensibly given a
roving commission. On 15 July 1915 he shot down another Morane
Parasol which this time was confirmed – Kurt Wintgens had officially
opened his score. On 9 August 1915 he accounted for a Voisin over

*Leutnant Kurt Wintgens at the wreckage of a BE2c he had just shot down. The body of the observer can be seen in the foreground, the pilot, who later died of his injuries, having been taken to hospital.*

*Leutnant Kurt Wintgens in the cockpit of his Fokker Eindecker wearing his glasses.*

Gondrexange, raising his tally to two and it was then that he fell ill with influenza and various other minor ailments, subsequently curtailing his flying. But on his return in January 1916 he resumed his scoring by shooting down a Caudron G.IV. By the end of June 1916 he had raised his tally to eight and was awarded the *Pour le Mérite*, only the fourth German pilot to be honoured with it. He was posted to FA 23's *Kek* Vaux, and then on to *Jasta* 4 when it was amalgamated. Three weeks later came another award, the Iron Cross 1st Class, which was quickly followed by the Knight's Cross with Swords of the Hohenzollern House Order and the Bavarian Military Merit Order 4th Class with Swords. His tally had risen by the end of September to 19 and with it came the award of the Saxon Albrecht Order, Knight 2nd Class with Swords.

On 25 September 1916, whilst flying escort to a two-seat reconnaissance aircraft, he fought off an attack by aircraft from the French *Escadrille* N.3 but in doing so was shot down in flames by the French ace Lieutenant Hurteaux. It is said that the observer in the German two-seat aircraft that Wintgens protected so valiantly was Josef Veltjens who was later to become a pilot and an ace. Kurt Wintgens was just 22 years old when he died.

### Oberleutnant der Reserve Kurt WOLFF
(1895–1917)

Kurt Wolff was born on 6 February 1895 in the village of Greifswald, Pomerania. At the age of 17 he became a cadet with Eisenbahn Railway Regiment Nr.4 where he served as an Unteroffizier in the field. On 17 April 1915, having seen action in the war, he was commissioned as a Leutnant der Reserve, but his eyes were fixed on other things and he asked to be transferred to the German Army Air Service. Although his regiment was reluctant to let him go, there was an urgent need for fighter pilots, his application was accepted in July 1915, and he was posted to *Jastaschule* at Döberitz. His first flight was nearly his last when his instructor misjudged a landing in their LVG, crashed and was killed outright but Wolff suffered nothing more than a dislocated shoulder. It did not deter him and he made rapid progress, receiving his pilot's badge and certificate in

December 1915. His first squadron was a KG unit at Verdun, where in his Albatros Scout he was quickly in action against ground troops. Some months later his unit was moved to the Somme where again it was soon in the thick of the action against Allied ground troops.

On 5 November 1916 he was posted to *Jasta* 11 where, although he carried out a number of sorties against Allied aircraft, he failed to score one victory. Then command of *Jasta* 11 was taken over by Manfred von Richthofen under whose guidance the *Jasta* began to take its toll on enemy aircraft. Within a couple of weeks Kurt Wolff had secured his first victory, BE2d No.5856 of 16 Squadron, RFC, over Givenchy on 6 March 1917. Within seven weeks he had taken his tally to an incredible 27. On 26 April he was awarded the Knight's Cross with Swords of the Hohenzollern House Order and a week later, on 4 May, the *Pour le Mérite*.

Leutnant Wolff.

*Portrait of Leutnant Kurt Wolff wearing his* Pour le Mérite.

His run of luck temporarily ran out when, on 11 July, after taking command of *Jasta* 29, he fought with a Sopwith Triplane from No.10 Squadron, RNAS, and was shot in the hand. Managing to fly his

*Fokker Dr.1, No. 102/17, in which Kurt Wolff was shot down and killed by Sub Lieutenant N M Macgregor of 10(N) Squadron, on 15 September 1917.*

Fokker with only one hand, he was able to return to his base. The injury kept him on the ground for two months but on 11 September he returned to the air and the following day orders came through announcing his promotion to *Oberleutnant*. On 15 September 1917, whilst on patrol near Nachtigal and flying in Manfred von Richthofen's Fokker Triplane, Dr.I 102/17, with other members of his *Jasta*, he encountered Sopwith Camels from 10 and 70 Squadrons, RNAS. After a brief dogfight, his Fokker fell to the guns of a Sopwith Camel flown by Sub Lieutenant N M McGregor, and he crashed just north of Wervicq. Kurt Wolff was just 22 years old.

### Leutnant der Reserve Kurt WÜSTHOFF
(1897–1926)

The son of a music director, Kurt Wüsthoff was born in Aachen on 27 January 1897. Even at an early age it was discovered that he had a natural aptitude for anything mechanical so it was no surprise when he joined the Army and immediately applied for the German Army Air Service at the age of 16. He was accepted and sent to the Military Pilot's School at Leipzig where, after four months, he was awarded his pilot's certificate and badge. But because he was too young to be sent to the front, Wüsthoff was posted to FEA 6 at Grossenheim as an instructor. After much pressure by his superiors, he managed to get posted to KG.1 in the Flanders sector. For the next 18 months Wüsthoff flew in such places as Bulgaria, Romania and Macedonia as a bomber/reconnaissance pilot and at the beginning of June 1917, after being promoted to Vizefeldwebel, he was posted to *Jasta* 4 in France. It was here that he scored his first victory when, whilst flying on patrol over Vormezeele, he attacked and shot down a Sopwith 1½-Strutter from 45 Squadron, RFC. Ten days later he brought down an observation balloon whilst over Wytschaete, for which he was awarded the Iron Cross 2nd Class.

At the end of July, with his tally standing at six, he was awarded the Iron Cross 1st Class. Kurt Wüsthoff was commissioned on 1 August

*Portrait of Leutnant Kurt Wüsthoff wearing his Pour le Mérite.*

JG I Staffelführers, L–R: Kurt Wüsthoff; Willy Reinhard; Manfred von Richthofen; Erich Löwenhardt and Lothar von Richthofen.

1917 and later that month, after scoring his seventh victory, was awarded the Knight's Cross with Swords of the Hohenzollern House Order. He continued to steadily take his toll of Allied fighters and by the end of November his tally stood at 26. On November 26 he was

The parasol wing Fokker D.VIII (initially designated the E.V.)

awarded Germany's highest award, the *Pour le Mérite*. He became acting commander of *Jasta* 4 in December until the end of February 1918 when he was promoted to Staffelführer. Wüsthoff was then assigned to the staff of JG 1 until 16 June, when he was given command of *Jasta* 5. The following day, whilst flying Georg Hantlemann's Fokker D.VII, he was jumped by fighter aircraft from 23 and 24 Squadrons, RAF, and shot down near Cachy. Badly wounded in both legs, he was taken to a French hospital.

Wüsthoff was released from prison hospital in 1920 and returned to Germany on crutches complaining that the French doctors had deliberately neglected to give him proper treatment and so he was taken to Dresden for German doctors to look after him. After a number of operations over a period of two years, he was finally able to leave hospital and walk unaided. He secured a job with an Austrian car manufacturer and was soon able to return to his first love, flying. On 18 July 1926 Wüsthoff took part in an airshow that had been set up to raise funds for a memorial to Max Immelmann, and during an aerobatic display he crashed and was badly smashed up. Five days later he died from his injuries.

# Glossary

| | | |
|---|---|---|
| AFP | *Armee Flugpark* | Supply Depot |
| *Bogohl* | *Bombengeschwader* | Bombing Unit |
| FA | *Flieger Abteilung* | Flying Section |
| FA(A) | *Flieger Abteilung Artillerie* | Flying Section Artillery |
| FEA | *Flieger Ersatz Abteilung* | Pilot Training Unit |
| FFA | *Feldflieger Abteilung* | Field Aviation Unit |
| Fr.v | *Freiherr von* | Noble family title of Baron granted by Royal decree |
| *Jasta* | *Jagdstaffel* | Fighting Squadron |
| JaSch | *Jastaschule* | Fighter Pilot School |
| JG | *Jagdgeschwader* | *Jasta* Wing |
| Jgr | *Jagdgruppe* | *Jasta* Group |
| *Kanone* | | German pilot with more than 10 aerial victories – equivalent of 'ace' |
| Kagohl | *Kampfgeschwader der Obersten Heeresleitung* | Combat Squadrons of the Supreme Commander |
| *Kasta* | *Kampfstaffel* | Fighting Unit or Section |
| *Kek* | *Kampfeinsatzkommando* | Fighter Group |
| *Kest* | *Kampfeinsatze Staffeln* | Home Defence Squadron |
| KG | *Kampfgeschwader* | Bombing Squadron |
| MFJ | *Marine Feld Jasta* | Marine Fighting Squadron |
| | *Ritter von* | Title awarded by Royal Decree |
| *Schasta* | *Schlachtstaffel* | Ground Support Unit |
| SFA | *Seefrontstaffel* | Marine Unit |
| SflS | *Seeflug Station* | Naval Air Base |

# Comparative Ranks

| German | British |
|---|---|
| *Generaloberst* | None |
| *General der Kavallerie* | General of Cavalry |
| *Generalleutnant* | Lieutenant General |
| *Generalmajor* | Major General |
| *Oberst* | Colonel |
| *Major* | Major |
| *Rittmeister* | Cavalry Captain |
| *Hauptmann* | Army Captain |
| *Oberleutnant* | Lieutenant |
| *Leutnant* | 2nd Lieutenant |
| *Fähnrich* | Officer Cadet |
| *Offiziersstellvertreter* | Warrant Officer or Acting Officer |
| *Vizefeldwebel/Wachtmeister* | Sergeant Major |
| *Feldwebel* | Sergeant |
| *Unteroffizier* | Corporal |
| *Gefreiter* | Lance Corporal |
| *Flieger* | Private |

| German Navy | British Naval Equivalent |
|---|---|
| *Kapitänleutnant* | Naval Captain |
| *Leutnant zur See* | Naval Lieutenant |
| *Oberflugmeister* | Naval Aviation Senior NCO |
| *Vizeflugmeister* | Naval Aviation Junior NCO |
| *Flugmeister* | Naval Aviation Airman |

# Classification of German Aircraft

| | | |
|---|---|---|
| A | | Unarmed monoplanes |
| B | | Unarmed biplanes for observation and training |
| C | | Armed biplanes for reconnaissance and bombing |
| CL | | Light C plane |
| CLS | *Schlachtflieger* | C plane for ground attack |
| D | | Single-seat armed biplane fighter |
| DJ | | Single-seat ground attack |
| Dr | | Single-seat armed triplanes |
| J | | Two-seater ground-attack infantry support aircraft |
| E | | Single-seat armed monoplanes |
| F | | First Fokker Dr.1s |
| G | *Grossflugzeug* | Twin-engined biplane bombers |
| R | *Riesenflugzeug* | Multi-engined armed biplane long range |

# Bibliography

Terry Treadwell & Alan Wood, *The First Air War*, Brassey's (1995).

Norman Franks, Frank Bailey & Russell Guest, *Above The Lines*, Grub Street (1993).

Bruce Robertson *et al.*, *Air Aces of the 1914–1918 War*, Harleyford (1959).

John Angolia & Clint Hackney, *The Pour le Mérite and Germany's First Aces*, Hackney Publishing Company, Texas (1984).

P J Carisella and James W Ryan, *Wie Richthofen Fiel*, Flieger Books (1954).

Peter Kilduff, *Germany's First Air Force 1914–1918*, Arms and Armour Press (1991).

# Index